Contents

Introduction

This book consists of fifteen extracts, mostly from modern novels, designed for pupils in the 11 to 14 age range. The passages are roughly graded in order of difficulty, with the last few selections coming from books aimed at adult readers. A synopsis is given to place the extract in context, and to stimulate interest in the text as a whole. Each extract is followed by:

- A series of comprehension/interpretation questions.
- A section headed 'Taking a Closer Look' focusing on one or more language features from the passage, with further explanations and practice exercises. The topics vary in difficulty, and teachers can use their own judgment in deciding whether a section is appropriate for a particular pupil group.

Additional material for revision is provided at the end of the book in an Appendix, the aim of which is to provide an extended glossary of technical terms with exercises to assist in acquiring understanding of these. Throughout this book there are also occasional cross-references to the authors' earlier textbook 'Knowledge about Language' to allow for more detailed exploration of aspects of language, particularly in topics specified in the 5–14 National Guidelines (Scotland) and Key Stage 3 (England).

MMF/AGR

GETTING STARTED

What is Close Reading?

Close Reading aims to test your understanding of language. You will be given a page or two of a story to read. Your teacher may read it aloud to you, or you may be asked to read it silently.

Then you will be asked questions which will make you think about what you have read. In the questions, the story may be called 'the passage' or 'the text'. Sometimes you will work alone; other times you may discuss the questions with a partner or a group. You will then have to write down answers to the questions.

What a shame!

You should think about what the writer is saying in the story and how you feel about it. The ideas might make you feel angry with someone, for example. Or you might find a story funny or sad.

What are the numbers down the side of the story?

These are line numbers. They are numbered in 5s. They help you find something in the story more easily. For example, if you are asked to look at line 17, you should find line 15 and then count down two more lines. Often a question will direct you to certain lines.

Look at lines 1–14

How does the writer present the situation effectively? . . .

Is there a right way to answer the questions?

Yes. The first and most important rule is to **use your own words**. Do *not* just copy out part of the text. The only exception to this rule is if you are asked to 'find a word in the passage' or if you are asked to 'quote'.

Do I need to answer in sentences or will one word do?

Sometimes a question will simply ask you to pick out a word or expression and a sentence is not required. If the question asks you to explain or discuss something, you should write in sentences, taking care with expression. Avoid beginning your answer with the word 'because'.

Will the questions be in any special order?

Usually, the answers will come in the order they are in the story. The first questions will deal with the opening paragraph, and so on. Often you will be directed to certain lines in the story to find the answer.

Why are the numbers of marks given after each question?

This is to help you. If a question is worth just 1 mark, one simple answer is needed. If the question is worth 2 marks, you will need to make two points, or answer in more detail. For a four mark question, you will need to write four times as much as for a 1-mark question.

What sort of things will the questions ask?

The questions will deal with two main things:

★ What the writer is saying – the **meaning**.

★ How he/she says it – the **style**.

What kind of things will be asked about in style questions?

Style questions deal with *how* a writer tells a story. You will be expected to comment on the writer's word choice and the use of figures of speech such as similes and metaphors. Things like sentence structure and paragraphing are also part of a writer's style. These topics are dealt with step-by-step throughout this book, and there is additional information with practice exercises in Appendix I at the end of the book.

Chapter 1

The Kingdom by the Sea

This novel by Robert Westall was published in 1990 but is set in the North of England in the 1940s at the time of the Second World War.

Extract

1   He was an old hand at air raids now.

 As the yell of the siren climbed the sky, he came smoothly out of his dreams. Not scared. Only his stomach clamped down tight for action, as his hands found his clothes laid ready in the dark.
5   Hauled one jumper, then another, over his pyjamas. Thrust both stockinged feet together through his trousers and into his shoes. Then bent to tie his laces thoroughly. A loose lace had tripped him once, in the race to the shelter. He remembered the smashing blow as the ground hit his chin; the painful week after, not able
10   to eat with a bitten tongue.

 He grabbed his school raincoat off the door, pulling the door wide at the same time. All done by feel; no need to put the light on. Lights were dangerous.

He passed Dulcie's door, heard Mam and Dulcie muttering to
15 each other, Dulcie sleepy and cross, Mam sharp and urgent. Then
he thundered downstairs, the crack of light from the kitchen door
lighting up the edge of each stair-tread. Dad was sitting in his
warden's uniform, hauling on his big black boots, his grey hair
standing up vertically in a bunch.
20 There was a strong smell of Dad's sweaty feet, and the fag he
had burning in the ashtray. That was all Harry had time to notice;
he had his own job – the two objects laid ready in the chair by
the door. The big roll of blankets, wrapped in a groundsheet
because the shelter was damp, done up with a big leather strap of
25 Dad's. And Mam's precious attache case with the flask of hot
coffee and insurance policies and other important things, and the
little bottle of brandy for emergencies. He heaved the blankets on
to his back, picked up the case with one hand and reached to
unlock the back door with the other.
30 'Mind that light,' said Dad automatically. But Harry's hand
was already reaching for the switch. He'd done it all a hundred
times before.
He slammed the door behind him, held his breath and
listened. A single aircraft's engines, far out to sea. *Vroomah,*
35 *vroomah, vroomah.* A Jerry. But nothing to worry about yet. Two
guns fired, one after another. Two brilliant points of white,
lighting up a black landscape of greenhouse, sweet-pea trellises
and cucumber-frames. A rolling carpet of echoes. Still out to sea.
Safe, then.
40 He ran down the long back garden, with his neck prickling
and the blankets bouncing against his back comfortingly. As he
passed the greenhouse the rabbits thumped their heels in alarm.
There was a nice cold smell of dew and cabbages. Then he was in
through the shelter door, shoving the damp mould-stinking
45 curtain aside.
He tossed the things on to Mam's bunk, found the tiny oil-
lamp on the back girder, and lit it and watched the flame grow.
Then he lit the candle under the pottery milk-cooler that kept the

50 shelter warm. Then he undid the bundle and laid out the blankets on the right bunks and turned back to the shelter door, ready to take Dulcie from Mam. He should be hearing their footsteps any second now, the patter of Mam's shoes and the crunch of Dad's hobnailed boots. Dad always saw them safe in the shelter, before he went on duty. Mam would be nagging Dad – had he locked

55 the back door against burglars? They always teased Mam about that; she must think burglars were bloody brave, burgling in the middle of air raids.

God, Mam and Dad were taking their time tonight. What was keeping them? That Jerry was getting closer. More guns were

60 firing now. The garden, every detail of it, the bird-bath and the concrete rabbit, flashed black, white, black, white, black. There was a whispering in the air. Gun-shrapnel falling like rain . . . they shouldn't be out in *that*. Where were they? Where *were* they? Why weren't they tumbling through the shelter door, panting

65 and laughing to be safe?

That Jerry was right overhead. *Vroomah. Vroomah. Vroomah.*

And then the other whistling. Rising to a scream. Bombs. Harry began to count. If you were still counting at ten, the bombs had missed you.

70 The last thing he remembered was saying 'seven'.

Questions

1 'He was an old hand at air raids now.' (line 1)
   a) What does this mean?   (1 mark)
   b) What shows he was well prepared for another raid?   (2 marks)

2 'Lights were dangerous'. (line 13) Why?   (2 marks)

3 '[Harry] had his own job – the two objects laid ready in the chair by the door.' (lines 22–23)
   a) Describe in detail what these objects were.   (4 marks)
   b) What did Harry have to do with them?   (1 mark)

c) Suggest a reason for taking any one of these items out of the
    house.   *(2 marks)*

4 'But nothing to worry about yet.' (line 35)
   a) Why did Harry think this way?   *(2 marks)*
   b) Quote a single word from anywhere between line 33 and
       line 45 which suggests that Harry feels quite at ease. *(1 mark)*

5 Name three things that Harry did as soon as he reached the air raid
   shelter.   *(3 marks)*

6 Quote the words which are the first hint that something is going to
   go wrong.   *(1 mark)*

7 Why did Harry think it was amusing that his Mum was worried
   about burglars?   *(2 mark)*

8 Suggest a reason why the author repeats the words 'where were
   they?' (line 63)   *(2 marks)*

9 What is the reader left thinking at the end of the
   passage?   *(2 marks)*

TOTAL MARKS: 25

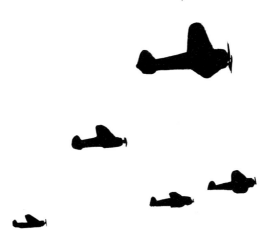

Did you know . . . ?

★ Between September 1940 and May 1941 Nazi Germany's air
  force (the Luftwaffe) launched 127 large-scale night raids on
  British cities
★ Over 60,000 civilians were killed and two million homes were
  destroyed

Taking a closer look . . .

Similes and Metaphors

When a writer is describing a person or a scene, he often compares it to something we are already familiar with so that we can form a clearer picture in our minds.

For example, the passage talks about

> Gun-shrapnel falling like rain.

Not many readers will have been exposed to gunfire, but everyone knows what rain feels like.

An expression which compares one thing to another and uses the word 'like' or 'as' is called a **simile**.

Sometimes, instead of suggesting that one thing is *like* another, a writer may simply make a comparison by saying that one thing *is* another. This kind of comparison is called a **metaphor**.

In the passage, the distant sound of the German bombers is described as

> A rolling carpet of echoes.

Here, the way that the muffled sound of the aircraft reaches the land is compared to a carpet. Why do you think that the writer makes this comparison?

For practice

Sort out these sentences into two groups – similes and metaphors.

Decide what is being compared to what in each case.

Discuss what the comparison tells you about the subject being described. In what way are the two things similar?

1 She was running about like a headless chicken.
2 I woke up in the morning feeling as fresh as a daisy.
3 'You'd better behave yourself! You're skating on very thin ice!'
4 Last night I slept like a log.
5 I didn't enjoy the party at all – I felt like a fish out of water.
6 Education is the gateway to adult life.

7   The poet Robert Burns wrote: 'My love is like a red, red rose.'

8   The teacher's ice-cold stare made the girl feel very nervous.

9   At last I've found the key to the whole problem.

10   What is it about Steve? He's like a magnet to the girls!

11   The fields were covered in a blanket of snow.

12   We tried to find our way but got lost in the maze of side streets.

For Further Study

More information and exercises on **Similes** and **Metaphors** can be found in *Knowledge About Language,* pages 117–119.

Chapter 2

Thimble Summer

Thimble Summer by Elizabeth Enright is the story of Garnet Linden and her brother Jay who live on a remote farm in the American Midwest. After a long period of summer drought, Garnet's parents are worried that the farm will be ruined. Then one day Garnet finds a silver thimble in the river bank and their luck immediately begins to change.

This novel was based on the writer's own experience of life on a farm in Wisconsin. It won the Newbery Medal which is awarded annually for the 'most distinguished contribution to American literature for children.'

Extract

1   Garnet thought this must be the hottest day that had ever been in the world. Every day for weeks she had thought the same thing, but this was really the worst of all. This morning the thermometer outside the village drugstore[1] had pointed a thin red
5   finger to one hundred and ten degrees Fahrenheit.

It was like being inside of a drum. The sky like a bright skin was stretched tight above the valley, and the earth, too, was tight and hard with heat. Later, when it was dark, there would be a noise of thunder, as though a great hand beat upon the drum;
10   there would be heavy clouds above the hills, and flashes of heat lightning, but no rain. It had been like that for a long time. After supper each night her father came out of the house and looked up at the sky, then down at his fields of corn and oats. "No," he would say, shaking his head, "No rain tonight."
15   The oats were turning yellow before their time, and the corn leaves were torn and brittle, rustling like newspaper when the dry wind blew upon them. If the rain didn't come soon there would be no corn to harvest, and they would have to cut the

Extract continued

oats for hay. Garnet looked up at the smooth sky angrily, and
20 shook her fist. "You!" she cried, "Why in time can't you let
down a little rain!" At each step her bare feet kicked up a small
cloud of dust. There was dust in her hair, and up her nose,
making it tickle.

Slowly Garnet walked to the yellow house under tall maple
25 trees and opened the kitchen door. Her mother was cooking
supper on the big black coal stove, and her little brother Donald
sat on the floor making a noise like a train.

Her mother looked up. Her cheeks were red from the hot
stove. "Any mail, darling?" she asked. "Bills," replied Garnet.

30 "Oh," said her mother and turned back to her cooking.

Garnet set the table by the open window. Knife, fork, knife,
fork, knife, fork, knife, fork but only a spoon for Donald, who
managed even that so absentmindedly that there was usually as
much cereal on the outside of him as inside at the end of a meal.
35 Then she went down to the cold room.

It was still and dim down there. A spigot² dripped peacefully
into the deep pool of water below, where the milk cans and stone
butter crock were sunk. Garnet filled a pitcher³ with milk and put
a square of butter on the plate she had brought. She knelt down
40 and plunged both her arms into the water. It was cloudy with
spilled milk but icy cold. She could feel coolness spreading
through all her veins and a little shiver ran over her.

Going in the kitchen again was like walking into a red-hot oven.

45 Donald had stopped being a train and had become a fire engine. He charged round and round the room hooting and shrieking. How could he be so lively, Garnet wondered. He didn't even notice the awful heat although his hair clung to his head like wet feathers and his cheeks were red as radishes.

50 Her mother looked out of the window. "Father's coming in," she said. "Garnet, don't give him the mail now, I want him to eat a good supper. Put it behind the calendar and I'll tend to it afterwards." Garnet hastily pushed the bills behind the calendar on the shelf over the sink.

55 The screen door opened with its own particular squeak and her father came in. He went to the sink and washed his hands. He looked tired and his neck was sun-burned. "What a day!" he said. "One more like this—" and he shook his head.

It was too hot to eat. Garnet hated her cereal. Donald whined
60 and upset his milk. Jay was the only one who really ate in a business-like manner, as if he enjoyed it. He could probably eat the shingles off a house if there was nothing else handy, Garnet decided.

After she had helped with the dishes, Garnet and Jay put on
65 their bathing suits and went down to the river. They had to go down a road, through a pasture, and across half a dozen sand bars before they came to a place that was deep enough to swim in. This was a dark, quiet pool by a little island; trees hung over it and roots trailed in it. Three turtles slid from a log as the children
70 approached, making three slowly widening circles on the still surface.

"It looks like tea," said Garnet, up to her neck in brownish lukewarm water.

"Feels like it too," said Jay. "I wish it was colder."

75 Still it was water and there was enough of it to swim in. When they were finally sufficiently waterlogged to be red-eyed and streaming, they went exploring on the sandy flats that had emerged from the river during the weeks of drought. They

80 wandered in different directions, bending over, examining and picking things up. The damp flats had a rich, muddy smell. After a while the sun set brilliantly behind the trees, but the air seemed no cooler.

Garnet saw a small object, half-buried in the sand, and glittering. She knelt down and dug it out with her finger. It was a
85 silver thimble! She dropped the old shoe, bits of polished glass, and a half dozen clam-shells she had collected and ran breathlessly to show Jay.

"It's solid silver!" she shouted triumphantly, "and I think it must be magic too!"

90 "Magic!" said Jay. "Don't be silly, there isn't any such thing."

¹ drugstore: shop selling refreshments and other things
² spigot: a tap
³ pitcher: jug

Questions

1 Write down a word or phrase from the first paragraph that shows Garnet does not like the heat. *(1 mark)*

2 Explain what is meant by saying the thermometer 'pointed a thin red finger' (lines 4–5). *(1 mark)*

3 'It was like being inside of a drum' (line 6)
   a) What figure of speech is used in this expression? *(1 mark)*
   b) Explain, using short quotations, how the comparison to a drum is continued in the next two sentences. *(2 marks)*

4 What was unusual about the thunderstorm described in lines 8–11? *(1 mark)*

5 Read lines 15–23. Explain in your own words TWO visible signs the drought was having on the crops and on the land. *(2 marks)*

6 "Oh," said her mother and turned back to her cooking. (line 30) Explain how Garnet's mother's speech and actions reveal her thoughts about the bills. *(2 marks)*

7 'Knife, fork, knife, fork, knife, fork, knife, fork but only a spoon for Donald . . .'. (lines 31–32).

Explain clearly why this piece of writing is more effective than just saying 'Garnet laid out four sets of knives and forks . . .'. *(2 marks)*

8 Look at the description of 'the cold room' in lines 36–42.
Do you think Garnet *does* or *does not* enjoy going down to the cold room? Pick out and explain TWO phrases from this paragraph to support your answer. *(4 marks)*

9 'Going in the kitchen again was like walking into a red-hot oven.'
(lines 43–44)
Explain TWO ways in which the writer has made this sentence effective in the story. *(2 marks)*

10 Read lines 55–58. Explain what you can tell about Garnet's father's mood from both his words and his actions. *(2 marks)*

11 Read lines 72–74. In what TWO ways is the river water 'like tea'? *(2 marks)*

12 What clue is there in lines 75–78 to explain why the thimble had not been found before? *(1 mark)*

13 Read lines 88–90: 'It's solid silver . . . any such thing.'
The words of Garnet and Jay in these lines show that their personalities are different. Explain the difference between the two children. *(2 marks)*

TOTAL MARKS: 25

Taking a closer look (1) . . .

Describing words

Adjectives add more information to nouns. Writers add them to descriptions of things to present a clearer picture; for example, a <u>thin</u> <u>red</u> finger.

For Practice (1)

Pick out the adjectives which are used to describe the following things in the story.

1 corn leaves (lines 15–16) _____ _____
2 stove (line 26) _____ _____
3 pool (line 68) _____ _____
4 water in the pool (lines 72–73) _____ _____

5 smell of sand flats (line 80)   _____   _____

6 thimble (lines 83–85)   _____   _____

Adjectives may also be used to compare things; for example,

fine   finer   finest

The grammatical terms given to these three forms are

positive   comparative   superlative

For Practice (2)

Can you fill in the blanks in this table? The words which have been filled in are all taken from the story.

positive	comparative	superlative
bright tall lively good	colder cooler	hottest worst

Adverbs add more information to verbs. **Adverbs of manner** describe *how* something is done. Most adverbs of manner end in the letters -ly.

For Practice (3)

In the following questions write down the adverb the author has used in each of the examples in part (a). (Some sentences have been simplified slightly.)

Then in part (b) suggest a *different* adverb of your own which would create a *different* effect in the story. For example,

a) Garnet looked up at the sky <u>angrily</u>. (line 19)

b) Garnet looked up at the sky <u>nervously</u>.

1 a) _____ Garnet walked to the yellow house.

   b) _____ Garnet walked to the yellow house.

2 a) Donald managed his spoon _____ .

   b) Donald managed his spoon _____ .

3 a) A spigot dripped _____ .

   b) A spigot dripped _____ .

4 a) Garnet _____ pushed the bills behind the calendar.

   b) Garnet _____ pushed the bills behind the calendar.

5 a) The turtles made three _____widening circles on the still surface.

   b) The turtles made three _____ widening circles on the still surface.

6 a) The sun set _____ behind the trees.

   b) The sun set _____ behind the trees.

7 a) Garnet ran _____ to show Jay the thimble.

   b) Garnet ran _____ to show Jay the thimble.

8 a) "It's solid silver!" she shouted _____.

   b) "It's solid silver!" she shouted _____.

For Further Study

More information and exercises on **Describing Words** can be found in *Knowledge About Language,* pages 26–33

Taking a closer look (2) . . .

Alliteration

Sometimes writers choose words beginning with the same sound to make a phrase stand out. In this story, Garnet's brother Donald's cheeks are described as being 'red as radishes'. Because the word 'radishes' also begins with 'r' it is more effective than saying 'red as tomatoes', for instance.

This technique is called **alliteration**.

There is another good example of alliteration near the end of the story, on page 15. Can you find it?

For Practice

Can you suggest an adjective to go with each of the following words from the story to form phrases with alliteration? For example, 'girlish Garnet'.

_____ Garnet		_____ heat	
_____ week		_____ lightning	
_____ day		_____ morning	
_____ sky		_____ rain	

Taking a closer look (3) . . .

Tone

Tone is the feeling which is evident in a piece of writing. In questions 6 and 10 on the *Thimble Summer* extract, you were asked to say what feelings the author intended to show through the words and actions of Garnet's mother and father. What you were being asked to do was say what the **tone** of their words was.

Tone can be made clear through word choice, and through other clues. Look again at these words from the end of the extract.

"Magic!" said Jay. "Don't be silly, there isn't any such thing."

We could describe the tone of this as **mocking** or **ironic** or **discouraging**. Jay's word choice of 'silly' shows that he finds

Garnet's belief in luck and magic ridiculous. He says dismissively 'there isn't any such thing'. The exclamation mark after 'Magic!' suggests he is jeering at her naivety.

For Practice

Say what you think is the tone of each of these pieces of direct speech from the text. Then say what clues are given. (There will always be at least one clue.)

1 Garnet looked up at the smooth sky angrily, and shook her fist. "You!" she cried, "Why in time can't you let down a little rain!"

2 After supper each night her father came out of the house and looked up at the sky, then down at his fields of corn and oats. "No," he would say, shaking his head, "No rain tonight."

3 "It's solid silver!" she shouted triumphantly, "and I think it must be magic too!"

Chapter 3

The Cay

The Cay by Theodore Taylor is set during the Second World War.
The word 'cay' in the title, which is pronounced 'key', is the word
used in the Caribbean regions for a small island. The story is
narrated by a young American boy, Phillip Enright, who at the
outbreak of the war is living on the strategically important oil-
producing island of Curacao, off the coast of Venezuela in South
America. This extract shows why Phillip's parents decided the island
was so dangerous that he should be evacuated to the United States.

The rest of the book is a story of survival and the overcoming of
prejudice. It deals with the extraordinary situation that arises when
the ship on which Phillip is travelling is torpedoed and sunk. Phillip
is blinded, and ends up on a tiny island with an old negro man who
is the only other survivor.

Extract

1   Like silent, hungry sharks that swim in the darkness of the sea,
the German submarines arrived in the middle of the night.

    I was asleep on the second floor of our narrow, gabled green
house in Willemstad, on the island of Curacao, the largest of

5 the Dutch islands just off the coast of Venezuela. I remember
that on that moonless night in February 1942, they attacked
the big Lago oil refinery on Aruba, the sister island west of us.
Then they blew up six of our small lake tankers, the tubby
ones that still bring crude oil from Lake Maracaibo to the

10 refinery. One German sub was even sighted off Willemstad at
dawn.

    The next morning my father said that the Chinese crews on
the lake tankers that shuttled crude oil across the sand bars at
Maracaibo had refused to sail without naval escorts. He said the

15 refinery would have to close down within a day, and that meant ➤

precious petrol and oil could not go to England, or to General
Montgomery in the African desert.

For seven days, not a ship moved by the Queen Emma bridge,
and there was gloom over Willemstad. The people had been very
20 proud that the little islands of Aruba and Curacao were now
among the most important islands in the world; that victory or
defeat depended on them. They were angry with the Chinese
crews, and on the third day, my father said that mutiny charges
had been placed against them.

25 "But," he said, "you must understand they are very frightened,
and some of the people who are angry with them would not sail
the little ships either."

He explained to me what it must feel like to ride the cargoes
of crude oil, knowing that a torpedo or shell could turn the whole
30 ship into flames any moment. Even though he wasn't a sailor, he
volunteered to help man the lake tankers.

Soon, of course, we might also run out of fresh water. It
rains very little in the Dutch West Indies unless there is a
hurricane, and water from the few wells has a heavy salt
35 content. The big tankers from the United States or England
always carried fresh water to us in ballast, and then it was
distilled again so that we could drink it. But now all the big
tankers were being held up in their ports until the submarines
could be chased away.

40 Towards the end of the week, we began to run out of fresh
vegetables because the schooner-men were also afraid. Now, my
mother talked constantly about the submarines, the lack of water,
and the shortage of food. It almost seemed that she was using the
war as an excuse to leave Curacao.

45 "The ships will be moving again soon," my father said
confidently, and he was right.

I think it was February 21 that some of the Chinese sailors
agreed to sail to Lake Maracaibo. But on that same day a
Norwegian tanker, headed for Willemstad, was torpedoed off
50 Curacao, and fear again swept over the old city. Without our
ships we were helpless.

A day or two later, my father took me into the Schottegat[1] where they were completing the loading of the *SS Empire Tern*, a big British tanker. She had machine guns fore and aft, one of the few armed ships in the harbour.

Although the trade wind was blowing, the smell of petrol and oil lay heavy over the Schottegat. Other empty tankers were there, high out of the water, awaiting orders to sail once they had cargoes. The men on them were leaning over the rail watching all the activity on the *Empire Tern*. I looked on as the thick hoses that were attached to her quivered when the petrol was pumped into her tanks. The fumes shimmered in the air, and one by one, they "topped" her tanks, loading them right to the brim and securing them for sea. No one said very much. With all that aviation fuel around, it was dangerous.

Then in the afternoon, we stood near the pontoon bridge as she steamed slowly down St Anna Bay. Many others had come to watch, too, even the governor, and we all cheered as she passed, setting out on her lonely voyage to England. There, she would help refuel the Royal Air Force.

The sailors on the *Empire Tern*, which was painted a dull white but had rust streaks all over her, waved back at us and held up their fingers in a V-for-victory sign.

We watched until the pilot boat, having picked up the harbour pilot from the *Empire Tern*, began to race back to Willemstad. Just as we were ready to go, there was an explosion, and we looked toward the sea. The *Empire Tern* had vanished in a wall of red flames, and black smoke was beginning to boil into the sky.

Someone screamed, "There it is." We looked off to one side of the flames, about a mile away, and saw a black shape in the water, very low. It was a German submarine, surfaced now to watch the ship die.

A tug and several small motorboats headed out toward the *Tern*, but it was useless. Some of the women cried at the sight of her, and I saw men, my father included, with tears in their eyes. It didn't seem possible that only a few hours before I had been

Extract continued

standing on her deck. I was no longer excited about the war; I had begun to understand that it meant death and destruction.

[1] Schottegat: harbour at Curacao

Questions

1 From the first sentence, suggest ONE reason why the German submarine attack would be particularly terrifying to the islanders.

(1 mark)

2 a) What figure of speech is used in the phrase 'like silent, hungry sharks'? *(1 mark)*

b) Suggest TWO ways in which sharks and submarines *are* alike and ONE way in which they *are not* alike. *(3 marks)*

3 Explain how the word 'tubby' (line 8) makes you picture the lake tankers. *(2 marks)*

4 In your own words, describe the action taken by the Chinese sailors after the tankers were sunk. *(1 mark)*

5 Explain exactly why the actions of the sailors had upset the people of Aruba so much. *(2 marks)*

6 Read Phillip's father's words in lines 25–27: "But ... either" and the following paragraph: 'He explained ... tankers.' (lines 28–31)

a) Why does he disagree with the people who were angry with
    the Chinese sailors?   *(1 mark)*

b) What does the whole of this section reveal about Phillip's father
    as a person?
    You should comment on:
    his attitude to the Chinese sailors
    his understanding of their task
    his volunteering to work on the tankers.
    You should quote from the text to support you ideas. *(3 marks)*

7 Read lines 41–44.
   Do you think Phillip's mother liked Curacao? Give a reason for your
   answer.   *(1 mark)*

8 'No one said very much'. (line 64)
   Why do you think people were so quiet?   *(2 marks)*

9 Read lines 66–70.
   How do we know that the departure of the *Empire Tern* was
   regarded as a great occasion?   *(2 marks)*

10 What can you tell about the morale of the sailors on the *Empire
    Tern* as they are described in lines 71–73?   *(1 mark)*

11 Read lines 77–79.
    The writer uses a metaphor to describe the exploding of the *Empire
    Tern*. Write it down.   *(1 mark)*

12 Read the last paragraph. Using your own words, supported by
    quotations, discuss in detail what this section reveals and suggests
    about how Phillip was feeling.   *(4 marks)*

    You could comment on some of the following phrases in your
    answer:
    ★ it was useless
    ★ men, my father included, with tears in their eyes
    ★ it didn't seem possible
    ★ no longer excited
    ★ I had begun to understand
    ★ death and destruction.

                                             TOTAL MARKS: 25

Taking a closer look (1) . . .

Nouns

Nouns are naming words. They can be classified in four main types:

Common nouns are general names of things. For example, ship.

Proper nouns are names of particular things or people. For example, Phillip.

Abstract nouns are terms expressing ideas or feelings. For example, fear.

Collective nouns are names by which groups of things are known. For example, army.

For Practice (1)

Draw a table with four columns, headed like this:

common	proper	abstract	collective

Then enter each of the following twenty nouns from the story into the appropriate column.

shark   darkness   house   submarine   Aruba
crew   gloom   Montgomery   victory   defeat
mutiny   torpedo   tanker   salt   excuse
voyage   boat   pilot   water   destruction

Fewer or less?

The word 'fewer' should always be used with plurals of those nouns which can be individually counted; 'less' should only be used with nouns which cannot be counted. A common error is to use 'less' with countable nouns. For example, this would be wrong: 'there are less girls in the class than boys.'

For Practice (2)

Draw a table like this with two columns, headed 'fewer' and 'less'. Then decide which of the following nouns should go into each column. Only those which **cannot** be counted should be put in the column marked less.

fewer	less

island   night   refinery   oil   petrol
gloom   defeat   bridge   shell   sailor
water   salt   vegetable   food   day
gun   harbour   rust   smoke   motorboat

When is a noun not a noun?

Some words can be used as nouns and also as other parts of speech such as verbs or adjectives. For example, 'rain' can be used as a noun: 'the rain was heavy' or as a verb (doing word): 'it began to rain.' (Verbs are explained in Chapter 4.)

For Practice (3)

Do this exercise in pairs.

In the following sentences the underlined words, which are verbs, can also be used as nouns. For each example, compose a sentence of your own in which the underlined word is used as a noun.

Then exchange your sentences with a partner and discuss how many you have got right.

1 The Chinese crews refused to <u>sail</u> without escorts.

2 Phillip's father volunteered to help <u>man</u> the lake tankers.

3 Phillip's mother was using the war as an excuse to <u>leave</u> Curacao.

4 Many others had come to <u>watch</u>, too.

5 The pilot boat began to <u>race</u> back to Willemstadt.

For Further Study

More information and exercises on **Nouns** can be found in *Knowledge About Language*, pages 7–13

Chapter 4

A Dog so Small

Just about every girl and boy goes through the phase of wanting a dog! In her novel **A Dog so Small,** Phillipa Pearce tells the story of a boy called Ben who is very disappointed when he doesn't receive a dog for his birthday. All he gets is a picture of one. At the time he has no idea what strange adventures this picture will lead to. . .

Extract

1   The post had come, and it was all for Ben. His father had piled it
by his place for breakfast. There were also presents from May and
Dilys, Paul and Frankie; and his mother and father had given him
a sweater of the kind deep-sea fishermen wear (from his mother,
5   really) and a Sheffield steel jack-knife (from his father). They all
watched while, politely, he opened their presents first of all, and
thanked them.

He was not worrying that there had been no dog standing by
his place at the breakfast-table. He was not so green as to think
10   that postmen delivered dogs.

But there would be a letter – from his grandfather, he
supposed – saying when the dog would be brought, by a proper
carrier, or where it could be collected from. Ben turned eagerly
from his family's presents to his post.

15   He turned over the letters first, looking for his grandfather's
handwriting; but there was nothing. Then he looked at the
writing on the two picture-postcards that had come for him –
although you would hardly expect anything so important to be
left to a postcard. There was nothing. Then he began to have the
20   feeling that something might have gone wrong after all. He
remembered, almost against his will, that his grandfather's
promise had been only a whisper and a nod, and that not all
promises are kept, anyway.

He turned to the parcels, and at once saw his grandfather's
25 handwriting on a small flat one. Then he knew for certain that
something was wrong. They would hardly send him an ordinary
birthday present as well as one so special as a dog. There was only
one explanation: they were sending him an ordinary present
instead of the dog.
30 'Open it, Ben,' said his mother; and his father reminded him,
'Use your new knife on the string, boy.' Ben never noticed the
sharpness of the Sheffield steel as he cut the string round the
parcel and then unfolded the wrapping paper.
They had sent him a picture instead of a dog.

35 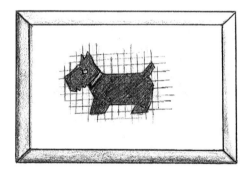 And then he realised that
they had sent him a dog,
after all. He almost hated
them for it. His dog was
worked in woollen cross-
40 stitch, and framed, and
glazed as a little picture.
There was a letter which
explained: 'Dear Ben, Your
grandpa and I send you hearty good wishes for your birthday. We
45 know you would like a dog, so here is one . . .'
There was more in the letter, but, with a sweep of his hand, Ben
pushed aside letter, packing-paper, string, and picture. They fell to
the floor, the picture with a sharp sound of breakage. His mother
picked it up. 'You've cracked the glass, Ben, and it's a nice little
50 picture – a little old picture that I remember well.'
'I think it's a funny birthday present for Ben, don't you, Paul?'
said Frankie; and Paul agreed. May and Dilys both thought it was
rather pretty. Mr Blewitt glanced at it and then back to the
newspaper he had opened.
55 Ben said nothing, because he could not. His mother looked at
him, and he knew that she knew that, if he hadn't been so old,
and a boy, he would be crying. 'Your granny treasured this
because it was a present from your Uncle Willy,' said Mrs Blewitt.
'He brought it home as a curio, from his last voyage – the last

> ## Extract continued

60 voyage before he was drowned. So you see, Granny's given you
something that was precious to her.'

But what was dead Uncle Willy or a woolwork dog to Ben? He
still could not trust himself to speak; and now they were all
looking at him, wondering at the silence. Even his father had put
65 the paper down.

'Did you expect a real dog?' Frankie asked suddenly.

Everyone else answered for Ben, anyway.

His mother said, 'Of course not. Ben knows perfectly well that
Granny and Grandpa could never afford to buy him a real dog.'

70 His father said, 'And, anyway, you can't expect to keep a dog
in London nowadays – the traffic's too dangerous.' Ben
remembered the cat scuttering from under the wheels of the car
that morning, and he hated his father for being in the right. 'It
isn't as if we had any garden to let a dog loose in,' went on Mr
75 Blewitt; 'and we're not even near an open space where you could
exercise it properly.'

Questions

1 What had Ben expected the postman to bring him on his birthday?

(1 mark)

2 Re-read lines 19 to 23.
   a) Why was Ben sure he was going to receive this present?

(1 mark)

   b) Give two reasons which suggest he should have been a little
      less sure. *(2 marks)*

3 Why do you think the writer uses the phrase 'there was nothing'
   twice? *(1 mark)*

4 What was it that finally convinced him that he was not going to
   receive the dog for his birthday? *(2 marks)*

5 a) How did Ben react when he saw what his grandparents' gift
      was? *(1 mark)*
   b) Give the reaction of any other family member. *(1 mark)*

6 'He almost hated them for it' (lines 37–38).
Why do you think he disliked this particular present more than 'an ordinary birthday present'? *(2 marks)*

7 Do you think Ben was right to react in this way? *(2 marks)*

8 In your own words, summarise Ben's mother's explanation of why his grandparents had given him this gift. *(3 marks)*

9 Why was it unlikely that the grandparents would have given him a real dog? *(1 mark)*

10 What TWO practical reasons against having a dog does Mr Blewitt suggest? *(2 marks)*

11 Explain fully Ben's TWO different feelings about what his father says. *(2 marks)*

12 Explain how in the course of the passage, Ben's feelings go through various stages, from hope and expectation to disappointment and anger.
In your answer you should:
★ Identify the various emotions Ben experiences
★ Refer to words or phrases from the passage to support your ideas. *(4 marks)*

TOTAL MARKS: 25

Taking a Closer Look . . .

Verbs

A verb is a doing word. It refers to an action, such as eat, drink, walk, sit, jump.

To find the verb in a sentence, ask yourself: what did the person who is the subject of the sentence *do?*

For example, look at this sentence from the passage:

> They all watched while Ben opened their presents.

What did *they* do?
What did *Ben* do?

'Watched' and 'opened' are the verbs.

Four things to remember about verbs

| 1 A verb is a 'doing' word. |

For practice

a) Write out the verb (doing word) from each of the following sentences:

1 Ben expected a real dog.
2 Ben pushed aside letter, packing-paper, string and picture.
3 Mr Blewitt glanced at the present.
4 Uncle Willy brought the picture home from his last voyage.
5 Ben said nothing.

b) From the list below, choose a suitable verb to fill each gap.

1 The shop _____ all the CDs in the charts.
2 Over the holidays I _____ one of the 'Harry Potter' books.
3 The postman _____ the birthday cards through the letter box.
4 Tracy _____ the most fashionable pair of jeans in the sale.
5 Kathleen _____ the shelving unit by herself.

read   picked   assembled   pushed   sold

| 2 Words like 'be' and 'have' are also verbs. |

To be: I am   To have: I/you/we/they have
          you are   he/she has
          he/she is
          we are
          you (plural) are
          they are

For Practice

Pick out the verbs from each of the following sentences:

1 The builder climbed to the top of the ladder.
2 I usually eat a bowl of cereal at breakfast time.
3 I slept till nearly eleven o'clock on Saturday morning.
4 He had ten minutes before the train arrived.

5　'Hurry up!' shouted my dad.

6　Alan has far more money than I have.

7　The ghost frightened the visitors to the lonely castle.

8　You are an only child but I have three brothers.

9　Craig scored two goals at last week's match.

10　Cabbage is not my favourite food.

DID YOU NOTICE that some of these sentences contain more than one verb? Go back and check again!

3　A verb can be made up of more than a single word.

The plane will be landing at about six o'clock.

Is the verb in this sentence *will?*
Or is it *be?*
Or *landing?*

Remember that the verb describes the **action** taken. The action here is that the plane *will be landing.* These three words are therefore the verb in this sentence.

For practice

a)　Pick out the verbs in the following sentences. Again, there may be more than one verb in each sentence, and often the verb will be made up of more than a single word.

1　I am going out whether you like it or not!

2　They have been trying for weeks without success.

3　You have seen that film four times already.

4   I will be fourteen on my next birthday.

5   I wonder if Partick Thistle will beat Rangers this weekend?

b)   From the list below, choose a suitable verb phrase to fill the gap.

1   We _____ on a world cruise next summer, but my parents haven't made up their minds yet.

2   Barry _____ by John.

3   I _____ home soon.

4   The detectives _____ for the bank robber.

5   My sister _____ since 8 o'clock this morning.

> *has been working*   *will be going*   *was being bullied*
> *are looking*   *might be going*

---

4   Verbs can be in different tenses.

Can you think why the extra words were added to the verb in the examples in the last exercise?

The job that the extra words like 'have been', 'might be', 'will be' and so on do is to tell you **when** the action takes place. This is called the **tense** of the verb.

In exercise 3b), decide whether the action
★ is taking place now (i.e. **present tense**)
★ has already taken place (i.e. **past tense**)
★ hasn't taken place yet (i.e. **future tense**).

For practice

a)   Copy out this table and fill in each box.

	SENTENCE	VERB	TENSE
1	At sunset we stopped at the top of the hill and rested for a while.	_____	_____
2	This looks like a suitable place.	_____	_____
3	Before we knew it, the sun was blazing down on us.	_____	_____
4	'What time is it?' I asked our guide.	_____	_____
5	'It will be eight o'clock soon,' he replied.	_____	_____

Check that you have found a total of nine verbs in these sentences.

> Remember!
>
> The verb will often be more than just a single word.

b) Pick out the ten verbs in the present tense in this paragraph.

Then rewrite the passage, changing all these verbs from the present tense to the past tense.

I wake up in a hot, dry wilderness. I remember that we desperately need water. I sit up and rub my grimy face with my hands and it feels like my eyelids and lips are stuck together. It is not far from dawn but there is none of the bright feel of sunrise in the air. The others are still fast asleep.

For Further Study

More information and exercises on **Verbs** can be found in *Knowledge About Language*, pages 13–26

Chapter 5

When Hitler Stole Pink Rabbit

The year is 1933, and Hitler has come to power in Germany. Anna, aged 9, and her brother Max, 12, are German Jews. The family has moved to Switzerland to escape the growing threat of Nazi persecution. However, the Swiss authorities are afraid of offending the Nazis and they will not allow Anna's father, a writer, to publish his work in Switzerland. Anna's parents then think of moving to France so that her father can go on earning a living. They leave Anna and Max in the care of Herr and Frau Zwirn, a kindly Swiss couple who keep an inn. The Zwirns have two children, Vreneli and Franz.

Extract

1 At the end of the second week after Mama and Papa's departure Anna's class went on an excursion into the mountains. They did not get back to the inn until evening. Then, although it was only seven o'clock, she went to bed. On her way upstairs she came
5 upon Franz and Vreneli whispering together in the corridor. When they saw her they stopped.

'What were you saying?' said Anna. She had caught her father's name and something about the Nazis.

'Pa said we weren't to tell you,' said Vreneli unhappily.

10 'For fear of upsetting you,' said Franz. 'But it was in the paper. The Nazis are putting a price on your Pa's head.'

'A price on his head?' asked Anna stupidly.

'Yes,' said Franz. 'A thousand German Marks. Pa says it shows how important your Pa must be. There was a picture of him and all.'

15 How could you put a thousand Marks on a person's head? It was silly. She determined to ask Max when he came up to bed but fell asleep long before.

In the middle of the night Anna woke up. It was quite sudden, like something being switched on inside her head, and she was
20 immediately wide awake. And as though she had been thinking of nothing else all night, she suddenly knew with terrible clarity how you put a thousand Marks on a person's head.

In her mind she saw a room. It was a funny looking room because it was in France and the ceiling, instead of being solid,
25 was a mass of criss-crossing beams. In the gaps between them something was moving. It was dark, but now the door opened and the light came on. Papa was coming to bed. He took a few steps towards the middle of the room. 'Don't!' Anna wanted to cry and then the terrible shower of heavy coins began. It came
30 pouring down from the ceiling on to Papa's head. She called out but the coins kept coming. He sank to his knees under their weight and the coins kept falling and falling until he was completely buried under them.

So this was what Herr Zwirn had not wanted her to know. This
was what the Nazis were going to do to Papa. Or perhaps, since it
was in the paper, they had already done it. She lay staring into
the darkness, sick with fear. In the other bed she could hear Max
breathing quietly and regularly. Should she wake him? But Max
hated being disturbed in the night – he would probably only be
cross and say that it was all nonsense. And perhaps it was all
nonsense, she thought with a sudden lightening of her misery.
Perhaps in the morning she would be able to see it as one of
those silly night fears which had frightened her when she was
younger like the times when she had thought that the house was
on fire, or that her heart had stopped. In the morning there
would be the usual postcard from Mama and Papa and everything
would be all right. Yes, but this was not something she had
imagined – it had been in the paper . . . Her thoughts went round
and round.

But at breakfast there was no postcard from Mama and
Papa.

'Why do you think it hasn't come?' she asked Max.

'Postal delay,' said Max indistinctly through a mouthful of
bread. 'Bye!' and he rushed to catch his train.

'I dare say it'll come this afternoon,' said Herr Zwirn.

There was still no postcard when she came home from school,
nor was there anything in the last post at seven o'clock. It was
the first time that Mama and Papa had not written. Anna
managed to get through supper thinking cool thoughts about
postal delays, but once she was in bed with the light out all the
terror of the previous night came flooding back with such force
that she felt almost choked by it. She tried to remember that she
was a Jew and must not be frightened, otherwise the Nazis would
say that all Jews were cowards – but it was no use. She kept seeing
the room with the strange ceiling and the terrible rain of coins
coming down on Papa's head. Even though she shut her eyes and
buried her face in the pillow she could still see it.

She must have been making some noise in bed for Max
suddenly said, 'What's the matter?'

Extract continued

70 'Oh, you idiot!' he said when she had explained her fears. 'Don't you know what is meant by a price on someone's head? It means offering a reward to anyone who captures that person.'

'There you are!' wailed Anna. 'The Nazis are trying to get Papa!'

75 'Well, in a way,' said Max. 'But Herr Zwirn doesn't think it's very serious – after all there's not much they can do about it as Papa isn't in Germany.'

'You think he's all right?'

'Of course he's all right. We'll have a postcard in the morning.'

80 In the morning instead of a postcard they had a long letter. Mama and Papa had decided that they should all live in Paris together and Papa was coming to collect them.

· · · · · ·

'Papa,' said Anna after the first excitement of seeing him safe and
85 sound had worn off. 'Papa, I was a bit upset when I heard about the price on you head.'

'So was I!' said Papa. 'Very upset.'

'Were you?' asked Anna, surprised. Papa had always seemed so brave.

90 'Well, it's such a very small price,' explained Papa. 'A thousand Marks goes nowhere these days. I think I'm worth a lot more, don't you?'

'Yes,' said Anna, feeling better.

'No self-respecting kidnapper would touch it,' said Papa. He
95 shook his head sadly. 'I've a good mind to write to Hitler and complain.'

Questions

1 Give ONE reason why Anna might be upset or alarmed when she finds Franz and Vreneli talking together in the corridor. *(1 mark)*

2 Explain in your own words why Franz and Vreneli don't wish to tell Anna what they have been saying. *(2 marks)*

3 What TWO things are we told were included in the newspaper article mentioned by Franz? *(2 marks)*

4 Read lines 18–20 'It was quite sudden . . . wide awake'.
   a) Explain in your own words how Anna feels as she wakes up.
                                                (1 mark)
   b) What figure of speech does the writer use in this sentence?
                                                (1 mark)

5 a) Read lines 23–33 'In her mind . . . under them.'
      Anna has a vision which she thinks helps her understand the meaning of the phrase 'having a price on your head'. Briefly describe her vision in your own words. *(2 marks)*
   b) Read lines 34–37 'So this . . . sick with fear.'
      Explain why you think Anna finds the vision so disturbing.
                                              (2 marks)
   c) Why does Anna believe this is more than just a 'night fear' (line 43) such as she had when she was younger? *(1 mark)*

6 In the morning, what fact seems to confirm Anna's fear that her vision might be coming true? *(1 mark)*

7 Read lines 58–62 'Anna managed . . . almost choked by it.'
Look at the author's word choice in this sentence. Comment on TWO words or phrases which you feel help us imagine the strength of Anna's feelings. *(2 marks)*

8 Read lines 62–64 'She tried . . . no use'.
Explain why Anna believes she has a particular reason to control her fear. *(2 marks)*

9 In lines 70–72, Max explains what 'to have a price on your head' really means. What is the real explanation? *(2 marks)*

10 When Anna's father returns, Anna confesses 'I was *a bit* upset'. Why do you think she does not say 'I was *very* upset'? *(2 marks)*

11 In your own words, explain Anna's father's response to the news he has 'a price on his head'. What does his response reveal about him as a person? *(4 marks)*

TOTAL MARKS: 25

Taking a closer look (1) . . .

Point of View

Judith Kerr, the author of *When Hitler Stole Pink Rabbit*, based Anna's adventures on her own early life, when her family, who were also Jews, had to leave Nazi Europe.

In the story, Judith Kerr writes in **the third person**. She talks of 'Anna', 'she' and 'her' and not 'I', 'me' or 'my' when she is presenting Anna's story. However, the story is told from Anna's point of view. Anna is the central character of the story. It is Anna's thoughts and feelings that we are allowed to share. We, the readers, never know any more about what is happening than Anna herself does.

For example, when her parents are away in France, Anna worries about whether they are safe. We only learn they are safe when Anna gets 'a long letter' (line 80). Another term for this is **perspective**. We can say the story is told **from someone's perspective**, in this case, Anna's.

Judith Kerr also uses the simple language of a child at many points, which suggests a child's point of view, although at other times she uses more complex language. The following questions will help you see how skilfully this is done, although you may have hardly noticed while you were reading the story.

For practice

1 What words are used to refer to Anna's parents? What effect does this have?

2 In line 15 there is a question. Who is asking the question? Is there an answer?

3 a) 'It was silly.' (Lines 15–16) How do the word choice, sentence structure and ideas in this sentence show that it is Anna's thought?

   b) Pick out a word from the next sentence that contrasts with this because it does not sound like a child's expression.

4 Look at the paragraph beginning at line 23: 'In her mind . . .' How does the description of the room suggest a child's simple view of things?

5 Look at the paragraph beginning at line 34: 'So this . . .' The following expressions can be divided into those which are presented as Anna's own thoughts and those which are simply part of the writer's narrative.

Make a table with two columns, headed 'Anna thinking' and 'writer telling', and put each expression in the column you think it belongs to.

Anna thinking	Writer telling

a) This was what the Nazis were going to do to Papa.

b) She lay staring into the darkness.

c) She could hear Max breathing regularly and quietly.

d) Should she wake him?

e) He would probably only be cross.

f) A sudden lightening of her misery

g) Yes, but this was not something she had imagined – it had been in the paper . . .

As well as imitating a child's simple language, a child's way of thinking is also suggested. Childlike thought is presented in many episodes, such as Anna's misunderstanding of 'a price on his head'.

The title of the book is a good example. When Anna's family left Berlin, they had to leave most of their belongings behind, including Anna's favourite toy, 'Pink Rabbit'. Anna imagines Hitler will take possession of her beloved rabbit. The title is therefore another example of one of Anna's own thoughts.

Taking a closer look (2) . . .

Symbolism

The title *When Hitler Stole Pink Rabbit* can also be seen as symbolic. **Symbolism** is when one thing represents or stands for another. The title suggests or 'symbolises' something about the treatment of Jewish children under the evil Nazi regime.

The **literal** meaning of something means the actual meaning. In the case of the title, this is comical, since we imagine Adolf Hitler in his Nazi uniform carrying off a child's pink toy rabbit.

However, this may **symbolise** the cruel way in which the Nazis often treated children in real life. Not only did they take their possessions, but also their freedom and in many cases their lives. Have you heard of Anne Frank, the girl who spent two years in hiding only to die in a concentration camp? Many Jewish children under Hitler's regime lost their childhoods. Anna is portrayed as one of the lucky ones who survived.

'A price on his head'.

Look again at Anna's vision (lines 23–33) which you were asked about in questions 5 and 9 after the passage. Discuss the following questions in your groups.

a) What literally happened in the vision? What did Anna think actually happened to her father?

b) Max explains to Anna the real meaning of the phrase 'to have a price on your head'. Consider what the fate of Anna's father could have been if someone had turned him in to the authorities for a reward.

c) Think of the similarities between your answers to a) and b). How might Anna's vision be seen as symbolic of her father's fate?

Chapter 6

A Series of Unfortunate Events

A Series of Unfortunate Events by Lemony Snicket sold over a million copies in the UK in 2002. There are now seven books in the series, telling the story of the problems faced by the three Baudelaire orphans – Violet, Klaus and Sunny. This extract comes from the first book, 'The Bad Beginning', and describes the three children's experience of meeting their unpleasant relative, Count Olaf.

Extract

1 I don't know if you've ever noticed this, but first impressions are often entirely wrong. You can look at a painting for the first time, for example, and not like it at all, but after looking at it a little longer you may find it very pleasing. The first time you try
5 Gorgonzola cheese you may find it too strong, but when you are older you may want to eat nothing but Gorgonzola cheese. Klaus, when Sunny was born, did not like her at all, but by the time she was six weeks old the two of them were as thick as thieves. Your initial opinion on just about everything may change over time.
10 I wish I could tell you that the Baudelaires' first impressions of Count Olaf and his house were incorrect, as first impressions so often are. But these impressions – that Count Olaf was a horrible person, and his house a
15 depressing pigsty – were absolutely correct. During the first few days after the orphans' arrival at Count Olaf's, Violet,
20 Klaus and Sunny attempted to make themselves feel at home,

Orphans,
To Do :—
Repair Windows
Repaint Porch

Extract continued

but it was really no use. Even though Count Olaf's house was quite large, the three
25 children were placed together in one filthy bedroom that had only one small bed in it. Violet and Klaus took turns sleeping in it, so that every other night one of them was in the bed and the other was sleeping on the hard wooden floor, and
30 the bed's mattress was so lumpy it was difficult to say who was more uncomfortable. To make a bed for Sunny, Violet removed the dusty curtains from the curtain rod that hung over the bedroom's one window and bunched them together to form a sort of cushion, just big enough for her sister. However, without
35 curtains over the cracked glass, the sun streamed through the window every morning, so the children woke up early and sore each day. Instead of a closet, there was a large cardboard box that had once held a refrigerator and would now hold the three children's clothes, all piled in a heap. Instead of toys, books, or
40 other things to amuse the youngsters, Count Olaf had provided a small pile of rocks. And the only decoration on the peeling walls was a large and ugly painting of an eye, matching the one on Count Olaf's ankle and all over the house.

But the children knew, as I'm sure you know, that the worst
45 surroundings in the world can be tolerated if the people in them are interesting and kind. Count Olaf was neither interesting nor kind; he was demanding, short-tempered and bad-smelling. The only good thing to be said for Count Olaf is that he wasn't around very often. When the children woke up and chose their
50 clothing out of the refrigerator box, they would walk into the kitchen and find a list of instructions left for them by Count Olaf, who would often not appear until nighttime. Most of the day he spent out of the house, or up in the high tower, where the children were forbidden to go. The instructions he left for them
55 were usually difficult chores, such as repainting the back porch or repairing the windows, and instead of a signature Count Olaf would draw an eye at the bottom of the note.

Questions

1 From the first paragraph, find another expression which means the same as 'first impressions'. *(1 mark)*

2 Quote the words which describe the Baudelaire children's first impressions of (a) Count Olaf and (b) his house. *(2 marks)*

3 Look at the punctuation used in the sentence in lines 13 to 17. What is the purpose of the dash after the word 'impressions'? *(2 marks)*

4 What two things mentioned in lines 26 to 27 made the bedroom unpleasant? *(2 marks)*

5 How did the children try to make the best of what was in the bedroom? *(2 marks)*

6 a) Which of the Baudelaire children do you think was the oldest or most responsible: Violet, Klaus or Sunny? *(1 mark)*

   b) Suggest a reason for your choice. *(1 mark)*

7 Find THREE more things mentioned in lines 34 to 43 that would make the bedroom an unpleasant place to stay in. *(3 marks)*

8 Find a word from the passage which means 'able to be put up with'. *(1 mark)*

9 In the words of the passage, give the THREE aspects of Count Olaf that the children disliked. *(3 marks)*

10 From your answer to question 9, choose ONE of these features and ·explain in your own words what it means. *(1 mark)*

11 What was the only thing about Count Olaf that the children did not mind? *(1 mark)*

12 Name TWO of the tasks he expected the children to perform. *(2 marks)*

13 How suitable do you think these tasks are for children? *(1 mark)*

14 Pictures of an eye are mentioned several times. What do you think this tells the reader about Count Olaf's attitude to the children? *(1 mark)*

15 In chapter one we looked at similes and metaphors. Find an example of a simile from the passage above. *(1 mark)*

TOTAL MARKS: 25

Taking a closer look . . .

Writing in sentences (1)

What is it that makes a group of words a sentence?

★ it is a complete statement that makes sense standing on its own
★ it begins with a capital letter and ends with a full stop
★ it contains a verb (a doing word)

For practice (1)

Imagine that a group of words was written on each of the rocks that Count Olaf left the children to play with. Sort out which ones are complete sentences and which ones are not. How can you tell?

1 Count Olaf's house was quite large.

2 Violet and Klaus took turns sleeping on the bed.

3 Instead of toys, books or other things.

4 The sun streamed through the window.

5 Violet removed the curtains.

6 If the people are interesting and kind.

7 Your initial opinion on just about anything.

8 The house was a depressing pigsty.

9 Without curtains over the cracked glass.

10 All over the house.

Creating more complex sentences

A story would make very dull reading if all the sentences were short and simple. Writers usually join short statements into longer ones. There are many ways of doing this, but one of the most useful ways is to use conjunctions (joining words).

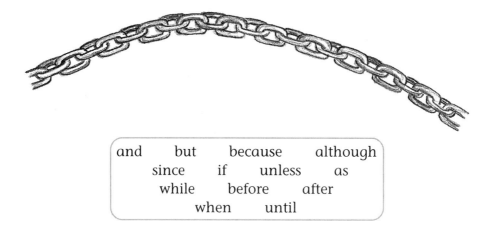

and	but	because	although
	since	if	unless	as
	while	before	after
	when	until

In the Lemony Snicket extract, many sentences are joined by using conjunctions.

Here, for instance, the writer might have used two short sentences:

> The children woke up and chose their clothing out of the refrigerator box. They would walk into the kitchen and find a list of instructions left for them by Count Olaf.

Instead, she puts the conjunction 'when' at the beginning of the first sentence and joins the two sentences into a longer one:

> <u>When</u> the children woke up and chose their clothing out of the refrigerator box, they would walk into the kitchen and find a list of instructions left for them by Count Olaf.

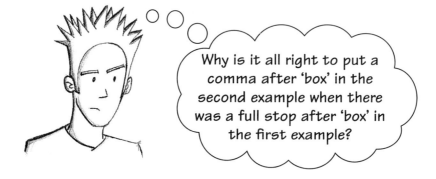

Why is it all right to put a comma after 'box' in the second example when there was a full stop after 'box' in the first example?

For practice (2)

Join these short sentences into longer ones by:

★ selecting a conjunction from the list on page 50
★ putting it in between the two sentences
★ changing the punctuation.

1 The orphans tried to get used to the house. They could not.

2 The early morning sunlight disturbed the children. They were still trying to sleep.

3 Violet made the curtains into a kind of cushion. The bed was very hard.

4 Klaus and Sunny soon became friends. They did not like each other at first.

5 The children felt very unhappy. Count Olaf came back home.

For practice (3)

Join these short sentences into longer ones by

★ selecting a conjunction from the list on page 50
★ putting it at the beginning of the first sentence
★ changing the punctuation.

1 The children lost their parents. They had to stay with Count Olaf.

2 The children met Count Olaf. They took an instant dislike to him.

3 Count Olaf's house was quite large. The three children had to share one room.

4 Count Olaf did not want to do them himself. He left the children unpleasant jobs to do.

5 Count Olaf had written a note to the children. He drew a picture of an eye on it.

For Further Study

More information and exercises on **Conjunctions and other methods of joining sentences** can be found in *Knowledge About Language*, pages 92–98

Chapter 7

Shoes were for Sunday (1)

Molly Weir was a Glasgow-born journalist and actress. The next two passages come from her autobiography, **Shoes were for Sunday**, in which she describes her childhood in the Springburn area of the city shortly after the First World War (1914–1918).

Rescue by tramcar

Up until 1962, public transport in the city of Glasgow was largely provided by trams which were powered from overhead wires and ran on tramlines laid in the middle of the roads. Here, Molly Weir remembers some incidents involving tramcars in her childhood.

Extract

1   One of the most dramatic stories told to me by my mother was of an accident to me in babyhood, when a tramcar was pressed into the rescue operation. I was about nine months old at the time and my mother had stood me up on the sink-ledge by the
5   window while she cleared up the bathing things before putting me to bed.

The china bath, washed and dried, was beside me on the draining board, and when I turned round at the sound of my father's key in the door, my foot went through one handle, and I

10 crashed to the floor. The bath broke into a dozen pieces, and an edge cut through the bridge of my nose like a knife. My mother used to shudder as she described the blood as 'spurting up like a well' but my father, quick as lightning, seized the two cut edges of my skin between his fingers, bade my mother throw a shawl

15 round me, and before she knew what was happening had dashed down two flights of stairs. He leaped on to the driver's platform of a passing tramcar.

'Don't stop till you get to the Royal Infirmary,' he ordered. The driver was so impressed with his urgency that he did exactly that,

20 and all the passengers were carried willy-nilly to the doors of the infirmary. To me the most impressive part of the story was that the tram wasn't even going near the infirmary on its route. It should have turned at right angles at the points long before then. I was astounded that a tramcar should have been used in this way

25 as an ambulance for me, and that the driver had dared vary the route from that marked on the destination board.

It was maybe this thrilling piece of Weir folklore which started my love affair with tramcars. When I was a little girl I only had the penny for the homeward tram journey, when my legs were

30 tired after the long walk into the town for special messages. It would have been impossibly extravagant to ride both ways. That luxury was only indulged in when travelling with Grannie, and the journey to town then seemed so different from the top deck of the tram, the landmarks so swiftly passed compared with my

35 usual walking pace.

When a halfpenny was laid on the tramlines it became a pretended penny after the tram had thundered over it and flattened it out most satisfactorily. To achieve this, we flirted under the wheels of the trams quite fearlessly, for we were so

40 familiar with the sight of them rocketing past our windows we saw little danger. I never knew any child to be injured by a tram. We were as surefooted as mountain deer, and the drivers were

> ## Extract continued
>
> quick to spot a faltering childish stumble on the rare occasion
> this happened, and to apply the brakes in good time. They'd all
> 45 played on the tramlines themselves when children, and our
> games didn't make them turn a hair. If a child was occasionally
> scooped up in the 'cow-catcher' – a metal shovel arrangement
> worked by the driver to remove any obstacle in his path – well,
> that was all right. Wasn't that what the cow-catcher was there
> 50 for? And it would be a good lesson for the youngster for the
> future.

Questions

1 In about 30 words, write a summary of the accident as described
   in the first two paragraphs. *(4 marks)*

2 What were the two things that Molly's father did immediately
   afterwards? *(2 marks)*

3 There are a number of similes in this passage.
   a) Quote two separate examples. *(2 marks)*
   b) Take one of the similes you have chosen and explain how good
      you think the comparison is. *(2 marks)*

4 Quote the phrase which explains why the tram driver did what
   Molly's father told him to do. *(1 mark)*

5 Explain what Molly later thought was 'the most impressive part of
   the story'. *(2 marks)*

6 Find a word or phrase from the passage that fits each of the
   following meanings:
   a) 'sudden, striking, full of action'
   b) 'stories from the past, handed down from one generation to
      the next'
   c) 'wasteful of money' *(3 marks)*

7 Re-read the last paragraph. In your own words, describe the trick
   that the children used to play on the tramlines. *(2 marks)*

8 Explain in your own words 'we flirted under the wheels of the
   trams quite fearlessly.' *(2 marks)*

9 Quote another expression that shows how confident the children were when they played this trick. *(1 mark)*

10 a) What is surprising about the attitude of the tram drivers to what the children were doing? *(1 mark)*
   b) Why did the drivers take this attitude? *(1 mark)*

11 Explain in your own words what the 'cow-catcher' was. *(2 marks)*

TOTAL MARKS: 25

Taking a closer look . . .

Genre

A genre is a type, or branch, of writing. For example, science-fiction, fantasy or romance.

Molly Weir's book belongs to the genre of **autobiography** – a word which is formed from three different Greek words:

auto = self   (as in *automatic,* something that works by itself*)*
bios = life   (as in *biology,* the science of life*)*
graphos = writing (as in *graphic,* which relates to the presentation of material in the form of drawings, diagrams or writing)

An **autobiography** is when *you* write the story of your own life.

A **biography** is when *someone else* writes the story of your life.

For practice

In this list you will find the titles of nine books, a short description of what they are about, and a list of genres. However, these are all mixed up. Sort this material out into a table as follows:

Genre	Title	Summary of Contents
Fantasy Crime Biography Autobiography Adventure Travel Science fiction Horror War		

Titles
The Hobbit by J R R Tolkien
Treasure Island by R L Stevenson
Murder on the Orient Express by Agatha Christie
The Hand of God: the life of Diego Maradona by Jimmy Burns
Learning to Fly by Victoria Beckham
A Farewell to Arms by Ernest Hemingway
The War of the Worlds by H G Wells
Notes from a Small Island by Bill Bryson
The Fall of the House of Usher by Edgar Allan Poe

Summary of Contents
The star tells the story of her life in the Spice Girls and her relationship with husband David.

The life of the famous Argentinian footballer who has been a key figure in four World Cups.

The classic novel of pirates and treasure.

The story of a magical adventure in Middle Earth and the quest with a powerful ring.

Gruesome story of a woman who is buried alive in the dungeons in an isolated mansion and who comes out of her grave.

An American journalist journeys through the British Isles and writes about his impression of British life.

Mystery about a passenger who is murdered on a train.

A story about the invasion of the Earth by creatures from Mars.

The story of a love affair between a soldier and a nurse during the First World War.

Chapter 8

Shoes were for Sunday (2)

'Entertaining Angels unaware'

In the second extract from her autobiography Shoes Were for Sunday, Molly Weir recalls her schooldays.

Extract

1 We always had Bible teaching first thing in the morning at school and one of the phrases which greatly puzzled me was 'entertaining angels unaware'. How could anybody be unaware of entertaining an angel, I thought? Surely they would be instantly
5 recognisable by their beautiful white wings and the clouds of glory round their heads? It never occurred to me that angelic qualities could be found in the most unlikely guises, hiding under very ordinary voices and in bustling everyday bodies.

My angel, as it turned out, hid inside the little figure of my
10 school-teacher, Miss McKenzie. To me she was always a little old lady, with her roly-poly plumpness, her slightly bowed legs, grey hair framing a round rosy face and caught up in an old-fashioned bun on top of her head.

She seemed so ancient that I was astounded to
15 hear her say one morning, in quiet explanation when she was a few minutes late, that she had been delayed waiting for the doctor to call to attend to her mother. Her mother! Surely she must be about a hundred!
20 Although I basked in Miss McKenzie's approval, I never really felt very close to her. We all held our teachers in some awe, and it never dawned on me to ask her advice as to what I should do when I left school. Surely there was only one thing to do? Get
25 a job and earn money to add to the household

purse as quickly as possible. But Miss McKenzie had other ideas. We in our house knew nothing of scholarships for fatherless children. The idea of a child from a working-class household going to college was the very stuff of story-books, and had

30 nothing to do with the business of living as we knew it.

Unknown to us, she bullied the headmaster into putting my name forward for a special scholarship open to children who showed some promise, and who would benefit from further education. As I was the school dux, he agreed, although he was a

35 bit worried about the expense of keeping me at college for a whole year from my mother's point of view. No earnings from me, and fares and clothes to be covered, for, of course, only the fees would be paid if I won.

Miss McKenzie brushed all argument aside. She came herself

40 with me to the interview with the scholarship board. To this day I can remember my utter astonishment when, on being asked if she felt I had any particular qualities, and would benefit from such a scholarship, this wee old-fashioned elderly teacher banged the desk with her clenched fist, sending the glasses rattling, and

45 declared in an American idiom I never suspected she knew, 'I'd stake my bottom dollar on this girl!'

I trembled at the passion in her voice, and at her faith in me. 'What if I fail her?' I gasped to myself. 'What if she has to pay all the money back if I let her down?' I knew we hadn't a spare

50 farthing to repay anybody, and I was sick with a sense of responsibility in case I ruined this new, violent Miss McKenzie. As I've said, I was a natural swot, but even if I hadn't been, the memory of that indomitable little figure would have spurred me on when I felt like faltering.

55 At the end of my year at college I was able to lay before her the college gold medal as the year's top student, a bronze medal as a special prize in another subject, twenty pounds in prize money, and a whole sheaf of certificates.

And suddenly as I gazed at her, and saw her eyes sparkling

60 with pride behind the gold-rimmed glasses, I realised how widely she had thrown open the door of opportunity for me. And I knew

> ## Extract continued
>
> for the first time what the phrase 'entertaining angels unaware' meant. For there, standing before me in class, was my very own angel, Miss McKenzie.

Questions

The answers to questions 1–3 can be found in paragraph one.

1 What puzzled Molly about the phrase 'entertaining angels unaware'? *(2 marks)*

2 Quote TWO features that she thought would make it easy to recognise an angel. *(2 marks)*

3 Quote the words which explain the meaning of 'entertaining angels unaware'. *(1 mark)*

4 In your own words, describe the appearance of Miss McKenzie, basing your answer on information in paragraph two. *(3 marks)*

5 What did Molly expect to do when she left school? *(1 mark)*

6 What did Miss McKenzie think Molly should do? *(1 mark)*

7 Why did Miss McKenzie's idea not seem a very practical one to Molly? *(2 marks)*

8 Explain in your own words: 'the very stuff of story-books' (line 29). *(2 marks)*

9 State two things that surprised the author about what Miss McKenzie did and said at the scholarship interview. *(2 marks)*

10 a) What worried Molly most about going to college? *(2 marks)*
    b) Quote a phrase which backs up your answer. *(1 mark)*

11 Find a word in the passage that means 'stubborn, unyielding, not giving up'. *(1 mark)*

12 'I realised how widely she had thrown open the door of opportunity for me.' (lines 60–61)
    a) Explain in your own words what this sentence means. *(2 marks)*
    b) Comment on the use of the word 'door' here. *[Hint: look back at page 10]* *(2 marks)*

13 This passage is written by an adult looking back on her childhood. Find one example (from anywhere in the passage) where the author is explaining what she thought or felt as a child. You can either quote or use your own words. *(1 mark)*

TOTAL MARKS: 25

Taking a closer look . . .

Writing in sentences (2)

a) We saw in chapter 6 that a sentence was a completed statement. But sentences can take different forms. In the previous extracts, Molly Weir uses at least four different types of sentence:

Statement: The bath broke into a dozen pieces.
Command: Don't stop till you get to the Royal Infirmary.
Question: Wasn't that what the cow-catcher was there for?
Exclamation: I'd stake my bottom dollar on this girl!

For practice

a) Decide whether each of the following sentences is

★ a statement

★ a command

★ a question

★ an exclamation

1 Surely there was only one thing to do?

2 She was a little old lady with slightly bowed legs.

3 We in our house knew nothing of scholarships for fatherless children.

4 What if she has to pay all the money back?

5 He was a bit worried about the expense of keeping me at college for a whole year.

6 Come here this minute!

7 I went out to the cinema last night.

8 Give that back to her.

9 Are you feeling any better now?

10 She is the most incredible person I've ever met in my life!

b) In writing which tells a story (narrative writing) sentences generally use either the first person or the third person.

First person ('I') is when the writer is telling the story from his or her own point of view

Third person (he/she/it) is when the writer is narrating what happened to other characters in the story.

For example:

first person narrative

> When I was a little girl I only had the penny for the homeward tram journey.

third person narrative

> The driver was so impressed with his urgency that he did exactly that, and all the passengers were carried willy-nilly to the doors of the infirmary.

For practice

1 From the extract above, copy out TWO sentences that are in the first person and one sentence that is in the third person.

2 Why is the use of the first person particularly suited to the genre to which Molly Weir's book belongs?

For Further Study

More information and exercises on **How sentences are made up** can be found in *Knowledge About Language*, pages 73–78

Chapter 9

On the Island

Iain Crichton Smith's book **On the Island** brings to life the pains and pleasures of a young boy growing up in a remote village near the seaside in the Western Isles of Scotland. In this extract two boys go out at Hallowe'en hoping to see a ghost . . .

Extract

1   "I'll tell you something," said Daial to Iain. "I believe in ghosts."

It was Hallowe'en night and they were sitting in Daial's house – which was a thatched one – eating apples and cracking nuts
5   which they had got earlier that evening from the people of the village. It was frosty outside and the night was very calm.

"I don't believe in ghosts," said Iain, munching an apple. "You've never seen a ghost, have you?"

"No," said Daial fiercely, "but I know people who have. My
10   father saw a ghost at the Corner. It was a woman in a white dress."

"I don't believe it," said Iain. 'It was more likely a piece of paper." And he laughed out loud. "It was more likely a newspaper. It was the local newspaper."

15   "Come on then," said Daial urgently, as if he had been angered by Iain's dismissive comments. "We can go and see now. It's eleven o'clock and if there are any ghosts you might see them now. I dare you."

"All right," said Iain, throwing the remains of the apple into
20   the fire. "Come on then."

And the two of them left the house, shutting the door carefully and noiselessly behind them and entering the calm night with its millions of stars. They could feel their shoes creaking among the frost, and there were little panes of ice on

25 the small pools of water on the road. Daial looked very determined, his chin thrust out as if his honour had been attacked. Iain liked Daial fairly well though Daial hardly read any books and was only interested in fishing and football. Now and again as he walked along he looked up at the sky
30 with its vast city of stars and felt almost dizzy because of its immensity.

They were gradually leaving the village now, had in fact passed the last house, and Iain in spite of his earlier protestations was getting a little frightened, for he had heard
35 stories of ghosts at the Corner before. There was one about a sailor home from the Merchant Navy who was supposed to have seen a ghost and after he had rejoined his ship he had fallen from a mast to the deck and had died instantly. People in the village mostly believed in ghosts. They believed that some
40 people had the second sight and could see in advance the body of someone who was about to die though at that particular time he might be walking among them, looking perfectly healthy.

Daial and Iain walked on through the ghostly whiteness of the
45 frost and it seemed to them that the night had turned much colder and also more threatening. There was no noise even of flowing water, for all the streams were locked in frost.

"It's here they see the ghosts," said Daial in a whisper, his voice trembling a little, perhaps partly with the cold.

50 The whole earth was a frosty globe, creaking and spectral, and the shine from it was eerie and faint.

"Can you hear anything?" said Daial who was keeping close to Iain.

"No," said Iain. "I can't hear anything. There's nothing. We
55 should go back."

"No," Daial replied, his teeth chattering. "W-w-e w-w-on't go back. We have to stay for a while. "

"What would you do if you saw a ghost?" said Iain.

"I would run," said Daial, "I would run like hell."

60 "I don't know what I would do," said Iain, and his words

seemed to echo through the silent night. "I might drop dead. Or I might . . ."

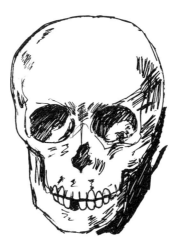

And then he stopped, for it seemed to him that Daial had turned all white in the frost, that his head and the rest of his
65 body were white, and his legs and shoes were also a shining white. Daial was coming towards him with his mouth open, and where there had been a head there was only a bony skull, its interstices filled with snow. Daial was walking towards him, his hands outstretched, and they were bony without any skin on
70 them. Daial was his enemy, he was a ghost who wished to destroy him, and that was why he had led him out to the Corner to the territory of the ghosts. Daial was not Daial at all, the real Daial was back in the house, and this was a ghost that had taken over Daial's body in order to entice Iain to the place where he was
75 now. Daial was a devil, a corpse.

And suddenly Iain began to run and Daial was running after him. Iain ran crazily with frantic speed but Daial was close on his heels. He was running after him and his white body was blazing with the frost and it seemed to Iain that he was stretching his
80 bony arms towards him. They raced along the cold white road which was so hard that their shoes left no prints on it, and Iain's heart was beating like a hammer, and then they were in the village among the ordinary lights and now they were at Daial's door.

85 "What happened," said Daial panting, leaning against the door, his breath coming in huge gasps.

And Iain knew at that moment that this really was Daial, whatever had happened to the other one, and that this one would think of him as a coward for the rest of his life and tell his
90 pals how Iain had run away. And he was even more frightened than he had been before, till he knew what he had to do.

"I saw it," he said.

"What?" said Daial, his eyes growing round with excitement.

95 "It was a coffin," said Iain. "I saw a funeral."

"A funeral?"

"I saw a funeral," said Iain, "and there were people in black hats and black coats. You know?"

Daial nodded eagerly.

100 "And I saw them carrying a coffin," said Iain, "and it was all yellow, and it was coming straight for you. You didn't see it. I know you didn't see it. And I saw the coffin open and I saw the face in the coffin."

"The face?" said Daial and his eyes were fixed on Iain's face,
105 and Iain could hardly hear what he was saying.

"And do you know whose face it was?"

"No," said Daial breathlessly. "Whose face was it? Tell me, tell me."

"It was your face," said Iain in a high voice. 'It was your
110 face."

Daial paled.

"But it's all right," said Iain. "I saved you. If the coffin doesn't touch you you're all right. I read that in a book. That's why I ran. I knew that you would run after me. And you did.
115 And I saved you. For the coffin would have touched you if I hadn't run."

"Gosh," said Daial, "that's something. You must have the second sight. It almost touched me. Gosh. Wait till I tell the boys tomorrow. You wait." And then as if it had just occurred to him
120 he said, "You believe in ghosts now, don't you?"

"Yes, I believe," said Iain.

"There you are then," said Daial. "Gosh. Are you sure if they don't touch you you're all right?"

"Cross my heart," said Iain.

Questions

1 a) What is Iain's attitude to ghosts?
   b) What is Daial's attitude to ghosts?   *(2 marks)*

2 Quote a line which explains why Daial has this opinion.   *(1 mark)*

3 The phrase 'Iain's dismissive comments' (line 16) means:
   (i) Iain did not take Daial seriously.
   (ii) Iain told Daial to go away.
   (iii) Iain agreed with what Daial said.   *(1 mark)*

4 What challenge does Daial offer Iain?   *(1 mark)*

5 Quote two separate words or phrases which emphasise how quiet the night is.   *(2 marks)*

6 What do we learn about (a) Iain's interests and hobbies and (b) Daial's?   *(2 marks)*

7 *Now and again as he walked along he looked up at the sky with its vast city of stars and felt almost dizzy because of its immensity.*
   (lines 29 to 31)
   Which word in the sentence above is a metaphor?   *(1 mark)*

8 Re-read lines 32 to 35.
   How is Iain's attitude to ghosts changing?   *(1 mark)*

9 What did people in the village believe that those with second sight could do?   *(2 marks)*

10 What does Iain think he sees in lines 63 to 66?   *(2 marks)*

11 Re-read lines 70 to 84.
   a) Write out three separate words or phrases that make the story seem particularly frightening here.   *(3 marks)*
   b) Quote the simile which describes how frightened Iain was.   *(1 mark)*

12 Daial has not seen the vision – only Iain. What is Iain frightened that Daial will think of him? *(1 mark)*

13 Iain *'knew what he had to do' (line 91)*
Write a short account of the rest of the story, explaining what Iain tells Daial and how he raises Daial's opinion of him as a result. *(4 marks)*

14 Quote a phrase which shows that Daial now has a greater respect for Iain than at the start of the story. *(1 mark)*

TOTAL MARKS: 25

Taking a closer look . . .

Direct Speech

Much of the passage about Daial and Ian takes the form of the actual words spoken by the characters. This is known as direct speech.

In a comic the actual spoken words might be put in a 'speech bubble':

However, when you are writing a story which includes conversations between people, follow these guidelines for the layout and punctuation of direct speech:

STEP 1

★ put the actual words spoken inside inverted commas (usually double inverted commas " ")

★ put a comma after the spoken words, but still inside the inverted commas. Add other words so that the reader knows who the speaker is (such as, *said Iain*)

★ then put a full stop.

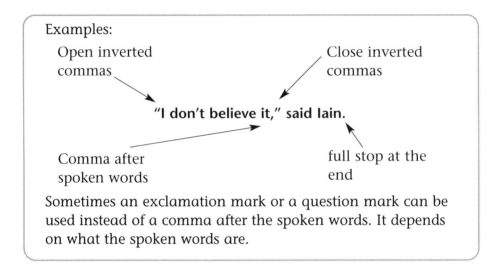

Examples:

Open inverted commas

Close inverted commas

"I don't believe it," said Iain.

Comma after spoken words

full stop at the end

Sometimes an exclamation mark or a question mark can be used instead of a comma after the spoken words. It depends on what the spoken words are.

"Did you see that film last night?" asked Amanda.

For practice (1)

Rewrite these sentences following the guidelines given above.

1 I'll tell you something said Daial to Iain
2 When are you going on your trip to Hong Kong asked Chris
3 I'm really looking forward to it said Tracy
4 I don't feel very well complained Craig
5 How about a bite to eat at Burger King suggested my friend

STEP 2

Of course, most conversations don't consist of single, short, simple sentences like these.

Look at this example:

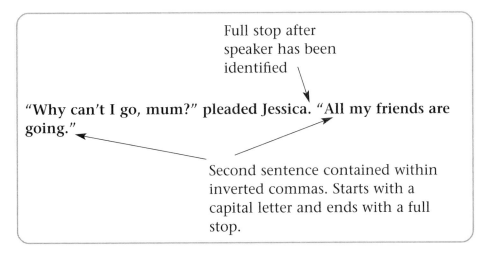

"Why can't I go, mum?" pleaded Jessica. "All my friends are going."

Full stop after speaker has been identified

Second sentence contained within inverted commas. Starts with a capital letter and ends with a full stop.

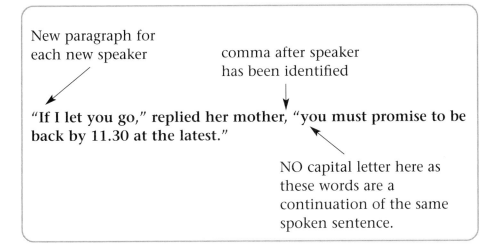

New paragraph for each new speaker

comma after speaker has been identified

"If I let you go," replied her mother, "you must promise to be back by 11.30 at the latest."

NO capital letter here as these words are a continuation of the same spoken sentence.

For practice (2)

To check that you understand the main rules for the use of direct speech, copy out the following sentences, selecting one answer from the alternatives in brackets. Look at the previous examples to remind yourself of the rules.

1 (*The actual words spoken / The verb of speaking and the name of the speaker*) are enclosed in inverted commas.

2 The punctuation mark at the end of the actual spoken words comes (*inside / outside*) the closing inverted commas.

3 When the actual words form a question (*a question mark / a comma*) is used before the verb of speaking and the name of the speaker.

4 When the actual words form an exclamation, (*an exclamation mark / a comma*) is used before the verb of speaking and the name of the speaker.

5 When the actual words form a statement, (*a full stop / a comma*) is used before the verb of speaking and the name of the speaker.

6 When there is a change of speaker, you should (*begin a new line / a new paragraph*).

7 If the same speaker continues after the verb of speaking and the name of the speaker, you should (*continue in the same line / start a new line*).

For practice (3)

Rewrite the following conversation which consists of sentences similar in pattern to the examples given above.

According to this newspaper report said Lewis Jack has been the most popular boys' name for the last eight years running

I though it would have been John said Emily

It used to be replied Lewis but John is now only number 62 on the list of the top hundred names

What's the most popular girls' name asked Emily

It's Chloe answered Lewis but I don't know any girls called that

I do said Emily there are two in my class at school where does all this stuff about names come from anyway she added

It says here explained Lewis that it's based on a survey of the names given to 160,000 babies born in Britain during the last twelve months

For Further Study

More information and exercises on **Direct Speech** can be found in *Knowledge About Language*, pages 106–108

Chapter 10

Paddy Clarke Ha Ha Ha

Paddy Clarke Ha Ha Ha by Roddy Doyle is about a ten-year-old Irish boy. The story is narrated by Paddy himself. Although Paddy's view of life with his little brother 'Sinbad' is very funny, the book has a more serious side, since Paddy also observes the break-up of his parents' marriage and his 'Da' leaving home. The title comes from the teasing words of his school-mates:

> 'Paddy Clarke
> Has no Da,
> Ha ha ha.'

Roddy Doyle won the Booker Prize in 1993 for this novel.

Extract

1   Liam and Aidan had a dead mother. Missis O'Connell was her name.
– It'd be brilliant, wouldn't it? I said.
– Yeah, said Kevin. – Cool.
5   We were talking about having a dead ma.
Liam and Aidan's house was darker than ours, the inside. That was because of the sun, not because it was scruffy dirty. It wasn't dirty, the way a lot of people said it was; it was just that all
10   the chairs and things were bursting and falling apart. Messing on the sofa was great because it was full of hollows, and nobody ever told us to get
15   off it. We got up on the arm, onto the back and jumped. Two of us would get onto the back and have a duel.

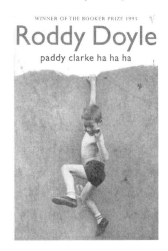

WINNER OF THE BOOKER PRIZE 1993

Roddy Doyle

paddy clarke ha ha ha

I liked their house. It was better for playing in. All the doors
20 were open; there was nowhere we couldn't go into. Once we were
playing hide and seek and Mister O'Connell came into the
kitchen and opened the press[1] beside the cooker and I was in
there. He took out a bag of biscuits and then he closed the door
real quietly; he said nothing. Then he opened the door again and
25 whispered did I want a biscuit.

I liked sitting in the hollow of the sofa, just back away from
where the shape of the spring was. The material was great; it was
like the designs had been left alone and the rest of the material
had been cut with a little lawn mower. The designs, flowers, felt
30 like stiff grass or the back of my head after I got a haircut. The
material didn't have any colour but when the light was on you
could see that the flowers used to be coloured. We all sat in it
when we watched the television; there was loads of room and
brilliant fights. Mister O'Connell never told us to get out or stay
35 quiet.

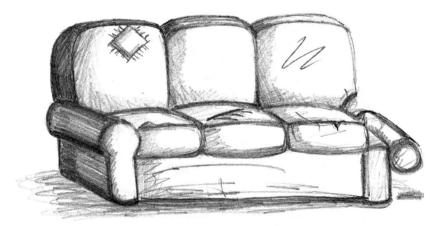

The kitchen table was the same as ours but that was all. They
had all different chairs; ours were all the same, wood with a red
seat. Once when I called for Liam they were having their tea
when I knocked on the kitchen door. Mister O'Connell shouted
40 for me to come in. He was sitting at the side of the table, where
me and Sinbad sat, not the end where my da sat. Aidan was
sitting there. He got up and put on the kettle and he sat down
again where my ma always sat.

Extract continued

I didn't like that.

45 He made the breakfasts and dinners and everything, Mister O'Connell did. They had crisps every lunch; all I ever had was sandwiches. I hardly ever ate them. I put them in the shelf under my desk; banana, ham, cheese, jam. Sometimes I ate one of them but I shoved the rest under the desk. I knew when it
50 was getting too full in there when I saw the inkwell beginning to bob, being lifted by the pile of sandwiches underneath it. I waited till Henno had gone out – he was always going out; he said he knew what we got up to when his back was turned so not to try anything, and we kind of believed him – and I got
55 the bin from beside his desk and brought it down to my desk. I unloaded the packs of sandwiches. Everyone watched. Some of the sandwiches were in tinfoil, but the ones that weren't, that were just in plastic bags, they were brilliant, especially the ones near the back. Stuff was growing all over them, green and blue
60 and yellow. Kevin dared James O'Keefe to eat one of them but he wouldn't.

I squeezed a tinfoil pack and it piled into one end and began to break through the foil. It was like in a film. Everyone wanted to look. Dermot Kelly fell off his desk and his head hit the seat. I
65 got the bin back up to Henno's desk before he started screaming.

The bin was one of those straw ones, and it was full of old sandwiches. The smell of them crept through the room and got stronger and stronger, and it was only eleven o'clock in the morning; three hours to go.

70 Mister O'Connell made brilliant dinners. Chips and burgers; he didn't make them, he brought them home. All the way from town in the train, cos there was no chipper in Barrytown then.

– God love them, said my ma when my da told her about the smell of chips and vinegar that Mister O'Connell had brought
75 with him onto the train.

He made them mash. He shovelled out the middle of the mountain till it was like a volcano and then he dropped in a big lump of butter, and covered it up. He did that to every plate. He made them rasher sandwiches. He gave them a can of Ambrosia

Extract continued

80   Creamed rice each and he let them eat it out of the can. They
   never got salad.

¹ cupboard

Questions

1 From lines 1–18, suggest ONE reason why Paddy envied Liam and
Aidan, although their mother had died.   *(1 mark)*

2 Using your own words as far as possible, explain TWO of the
games the boys played on the old sofa.   *(2 marks)*

3 In lines 20–25, Mr O'Connell finds Paddy hiding in his kitchen
cupboard. What was his reaction, and why do you think Paddy was
surprised by it?   *(2 marks)*

4 In lines 26–32, Paddy describes the old sofa in great detail. Choose
TWO of his expressions and explain how each helps you to
understand what the sofa was like.   *(4 marks)*

5 'Mr O'Connell never told us to get out or stay quiet.' (lines 34–35?)
Can you suggest ONE reason why Paddy tells us this.   *(1 mark)*

6 'I didn't like that' (line 44)
  a) Why do you think Paddy feels this way about what Aidan is
    doing and where he is sitting?   *(2 marks)*
  b) Explain ONE technique the writer uses in line 44 ('I didn't like
    that') to show the strength of Paddy's feelings.   *(1 mark)*

7 'They had crisps every lunch; all I ever had was sandwiches.'
(lines 46–47)
  a) Which does Paddy prefer – crisps or sandwiches?   *(1 mark)*
  b) Write down the expression which makes it clear which he
    prefers.   *(1 mark)*

8 How did Paddy know it was time to clear out the old sandwiches
from his desk?   *(1 mark)*

9 Who do you think Henno (line 52) is? Give a reason for your
answer.   *(2 marks)*

10 What do you think is the 'stuff' mentioned in line 59?   *(1 mark)*

11 Explain TWO pieces of evidence that show the reaction of Paddy's class-mates as he clears out his desk.   *(2 marks)*

12 Apart from the foods themselves, explain TWO aspects of the O'Connells' eating habits which Paddy admires and envies.
                                                                (2 marks)

13 What do you think is Paddy's mother's attitude to the O'Connells and the food they eat? How can we tell?   *(2 marks)*

TOTAL MARKS: 25

Taking a closer look . . .

Colloquial language

The word **colloquial** is derived from a Latin word meaning 'to speak'. It describes the type of language we use in everyday speech.

In his novel, *Paddy Clarke Ha Ha Ha*, Roddy Doyle cleverly gives the impression of the speech and thoughts of the ten-year-old Irish boy who is the narrator of the story.

For Practice (1)

Can you find one or more examples from the passage of the following typical features of colloquial language? One example of each is given to start you off.

Feature	Example	Your examples
Abbreviations	It'd (short for 'it would')	
Slang expressions	Yeah	
Use of first person	We were talking	
Personal opinion/feelings	Messing on the sofa was great	
Simple sentence structures	I liked their house	
Simple expressions rather than more technical terms	One of these straw ones	

For Practice (2)

Another typical feature of colloquial language is repetition. In formal language, we try to avoid this.

One of Paddy's favourite adjectives is 'brilliant'.

Can you suggest an alternative word or expression to 'brilliant' in the following sentences? Try to use a different one each time.

1 When we were on holiday in Spain the weather was **brilliant**.
2 *Gladiator* was a **brilliant** film.
3 My friend's Prada sandals are **brilliant**.
4 Mr O'Connell made **brilliant** dinners.
5 It would be **brilliant** to go to Mars in a rocket.
6 My sister is **brilliant** at gymnastics.
7 The boys had a **brilliant** time jumping on the old sofa.
8 Paddy's friends thought the mouldy sandwiches were **brilliant**.

For Further Study

More information and exercises on **formal and colloquial expression** can be found in *Knowledge About Language*, pages 112–113

Chapter 11

The Wind Singer

The Wind Singer by William Nicholson is a fantasy novel. Published in 2001, it won the 'Smarties' prize for the best children's fiction of the year.

Kestrel and Bowman Hath are twins who can communicate telepathically. They set off on a quest which will enable them to find the 'wind singer', a device which will restore harmony and freedom to their country which is in the grip of a cruel dictatorship. After Kestrel gets into trouble with the authorities who have sentenced her to be detained in a special school, she and Bowman escape from their pursuers by jumping down a manhole into the sewers. Here, a new menace awaits them.

Extract

1   They made their way along the tunnel, up to their ankles in
    water, and slowly the light from the open shaft down which they
    had come faded into darkness. They walked steadily on, for what
    seemed like a very long time.
5   All at once the tunnel emerged into a long cave, through the
    middle of which ran a fast-flowing river. The light which faintly

illuminated the glistening cave walls came from a low wide hole at the far end, through which the river plunged out of sight. The tunnel water now drained away to join the river, and they found

10 themselves on a smooth bank of dry rock.

Almost at once, Bowman felt something terrible, very close by.

'We can't stop here,' he said. 'We must go, quickly.'

'Where are you?' said Kestrel. 'I can't see you.'

In answer, there came the hiss of a match being struck, and

15 then a bright arc of flame as a burning torch curved through the air to land on the ground a few feet away from them. It lay there, hissing and crackling, throwing out a circle of amber light. Out of the darkness stepped a small figure with white hair. He walked with the slow steps of a little old man, but as he came closer to

20 the flickering light they saw that he was a boy of about their own age: only his hair was completely white, and his skin was dry and wrinkly. He stood there gazing steadily at them and then he spoke.

It was the deep voice they had heard before, the voice of an

25 old man. The effect of this worn and husky voice coming from the child's body was peculiarly frightening.

'The old children,' said Kestrel. 'The ones I saw before.'

'We were so looking forward to having you join our class,' said the white-haired child. 'Follow me and I'll lead you back.'

30 'We're not going back,' said Kestrel.

'Not going back?' The soothing voice made her defiance sound childish. 'Don't you understand? Without my help, you'll never find the way out of here. You will die here.'

There was a sound of laughter in the darkness. The white-

35 haired child smiled.

'My friends find that amusing.' And into the pool of light, one by one, stepped other children, some white-haired like himself, some bald, all prematurely aged. At first it seemed there were only a few, but more and more came shuffling out of the shadows, first

40 ten, then twenty, then thirty and more. Bowman stared at them, and shivered.

'We're your little helpers,' said the white-haired child. And all the old children laughed again, with the deep rumbling laughter of grown-ups. 'You help us, and we'll help you. That's fair, isn't it?'

45 He took a step closer, with little shuffling steps. As they came, they too reached out their hands. They didn't seem aggressive, so much as curious.

'My friends want to stroke you,' said their leader, his voice sounding deep and soft and far away.

50 Bowman was so frightened that the only thought in his head was how to get away. He stepped back, out of reach of the fluttering arms. But behind him now was the river, flowing rapidly towards its underground hole. The old children shuffled closer, and he felt a hand brush his arm. As it did so, an

55 unfamiliar sensation swept through him: it was as if some of his strength had been sucked out of him, leaving him tired and sleepy.

Kess! He called silently, desperately. *Help me!*

'Get away from him!' cried Kestrel.

60 She stepped boldly forward and swung one arm at the white-haired child, meaning to knock him to the ground. But as her fist touched his body, the blow weakened, and she felt her arm go limp. She swung at him again, and she felt herself grow weaker still. The air round her seemed to become thick and squashy, and

65 sound grew far away, and blurred.

Bo! She called to him. *Something's happening to me.*

Bowman could see her falling to her knees, and could feel the overwhelming weariness that was taking possession of her body. He knew he should go to her help, but he was frozen:

70 immobilised by terror.

Come away, Kess, he pleaded. *Come away.*

I can't.

He knew it, he could feel it. She was growing faint, as if already the old children were carrying her away.

75 *I can't move, Bo. Help me.*

He watched them gather round her, but he was sick with fear, and he did nothing; and knowing he was doing nothing, he wept for shame.

> ## Extract continued
>
> Suddenly there came a crash and a splash, and something
> 80 came charging out of the tunnel behind them. It roared like a
> wild animal, and struck out on all sides with wind-milling arms.
> The old children jumped back in alarm. The whirlwind passed
> Bowman, pushing him off the bank and into the fast-moving
> river. Kestrel felt herself being dragged to the river's edge, and
> 85 toppled into the water.
>
> The cold water revived Kestrel, and she began to kick. Forcing
> herself to the surface, she gulped air. Then she saw the low roof of
> rock approaching, and ducked back down under water, and was
> sucked through the hole. A few moments of raging water, and
> 90 suddenly she was flying through air and spray, and falling, falling
> with the streams of water, down and down, fighting for breath,
> thinking, this is the end, this is the smash, when all at once, with
> a plop and a long yielding hiss, she found she had landed in soft
> deep mud.

Questions

1 Read lines 1–4. 'They made . . . time'.
  Explain TWO things which made walking along the tunnel difficult.
  (2 marks)

2 Read lines 5–10. 'All at once . . . rock.'
  What TWO further dangers did the cave hold? *(2 marks)*

3 What does the word 'glistening' (line 7) tell us about the walls of
  the cave? *(1 mark)*

4 Read lines 17–22. 'Out of the darkness . . . wrinkly.'
  In your own words, explain what was strange about the child they
  met in the cave. *(2 marks)*

5 Read lines 24–26. 'It was . . . frightening.'
  Why did the twins find the child's voice specially frightening?
  (2 marks)

6 Read lines 31–33. 'Not going back? . . . You will die here.'
  Which TWO of the following words best describe the tone of the
  child's speech:

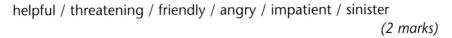

helpful / threatening / friendly / angry / impatient / sinister

(2 marks)

7 What does the word 'shuffling' (line 39) tell us about the way the children were walking? *(1 mark)*

8 'They didn't seem aggressive as much as curious'. (lines 46–47) Explain in your own words the meaning of this sentence. *(2 marks)*

9 Look at lines 53–58. 'The old children . . . *Help me.*' Explain the effect the touch of the old children has on both Bowman and Kestrel. *(2 marks)*

10 Read lines 79–81. 'Suddenly . . . arms.' Pick out THREE words or expressions which describe the 'something' which rushes out of the tunnel and explain what sort of creature these words lead you to imagine. *(3 marks)*

11 Look at the last paragraph. Explain in your own words how it helped Kestrel when she was knocked into the water. *(1 mark)*

Use information from the **whole** passage for the next two questions:

12 Which of the twins seems to you to be the braver of the two? Explain at least TWO pieces of evidence, and include short quotations from the passage as evidence for your opinion.

(4 marks)

13 In this extract, some conversations are in inverted commas and others are in italics. Can you suggest a reason for this? *(1 mark)*

TOTAL MARKS: 25

Taking a closer look (1) . . .

Onomatopoeia

Since this episode of the story takes place in the dark, the sense of hearing is important. The writer uses many words which refer to sounds.

Onomatopoeia is the figure of speech in which the sound of a word imitates the meaning.

For example, the word 'buzz' imitates the sound of a bee.

For Practice

In the following exercise you are asked **either** to find the example of onomatopoeia from the story which matches the word, **or** else to find the word or words from the story which matches the example. Fill in the table or copy it into your work-book. The first example is done for you.

Word / Expression	Onomatopoeia
1. the match being struck	**hiss**
2.	hissing
3.	crackling
4.	husky
5. old children's feet	....
6.	rumbling
7. 'something' charging out of the tunnel	....
8.	roared
9. heavy fall (which Kestrel expects)	....
10	plop; hiss

Chapter 12

Ash Road

Ash Road by Ivan Southall, is set in Australia. At the beginning of the story three careless teenagers start a bush fire while they are camping.

The novel was voted 'Book of the Year' by the Children's Book Council of Australia in its first year of publication.

Extract

1   It was early for Grandpa Tanner to be out of bed. He was up early
because the heat was stifling, and the sun was already glaring, and
the north-west wind that had blown all night was still searing[1]
the leaves off the trees as it had seared them the day before.
5   Grandpa hated the north wind. He had hated it all his life. It was
an evil wind, a wind that angered men and dismayed women and
frightened small children. The long grass growing up to the house
was as dry as straw, and dust was in the air, and the smell of
smoke. It was the smell of smoke more than anything that had
10   got Grandpa out of bed and out of doors in his pyjamas.

He could see no smoke in the sky, but it was in his nostrils, teasing them, and in his mind, in a way, prompting his memory back down the years to that one desperate hour when he had faced an inferno on his own and fought it on his own and beaten

15 it on his own. He had prayed hard at the time, prayed for a wind-change, for rain, for an army of men with beaters; but none of these had come, and he had done it on his own, and had stood blackened and burnt and bare-headed in the paddock, in the prime of his strength, shaking his fist at the heavens.

20 An old bushman like Grandpa could smell eucalyptus smoke on the wind from a fire burning fifteen or twenty miles away; he could smell it and feel it and see it with his eyes shut, with tingling senses, with an awareness that was electric. He stood almost motionless, every part of him tuned to that faint signal of

25 smoke.

Not in years had Grandpa seen real smoke – the savage, boiling, black-red smoke of a forest fire on the rampage. He had seen the smoke of scrub fires that had got a little out of hand for an hour or two; the smoke when farmers burnt off new ground, or

30 when shire-workers burnt off the roadsides; and the smoke when fire brigades were cleaning up hazardous pockets of bush before the full heat of summer (the boys of the fire brigades enjoyed a good blaze now and then). But he hadn't seen real smoke close to home since 1913. He had read of bad fires and seen far-off glows

35 in the sky by night, particularly in 1939, but those days seemed to have gone; there were too many people now.

Though the presence of fire always frightened him, Grandpa had never been unduly afraid of it. He knew that fires, unlike earthquakes or avalanches or erupting volcanoes, could be

40 stopped or turned. Men who knew what they were doing could even fight fire with fire. That was what Grandpa had done in 1913, and he had saved his farm though others not so far away had been wiped out. Even the township of Prescott had gone that day, 13th January. It had been there in the morning, and in the

45 afternoon it was a heap of charred rubbish and the Gibson family had been burnt to death.

Extract continued

That dreadful day had started like this one, even to the date of
the month – the same searing northerly, the same faint smell of
smoke, the same sort of temperature that had climbed and
50 climbed to over 112 degrees in the shade. And when the fire had
come over the top of the range and thundered into the valley like
a thousand locomotives steaming abreast, it had become still
hotter and hotter – so hot that birds on the wing fell dead and
grass started burning almost of its own accord and locked up
55 houses exploded and creeks boiled.

But that had been a long time ago. It couldn't happen now.

[1]searing – burning

Questions

1 a) What is the main reason given in the first paragraph for
        Grandpa Tanner being up and out so early?   *(1 mark)*
    b) Quote the expression that shows this was the main reason,
        although there were other reasons.   *(1 mark)*

2 Read lines 5–7. In your own words, explain the different feelings
   people had about the north wind.   *(3 marks)*

3 What piece of information given in paragraph one suggests that
   this would be a very dangerous time for a fire to start? Explain your
   answer.   *(2 marks)*

4 Explain clearly, using quotations, how the writer has used
   repetition in the second paragraph to make the story of the earlier
   fire dramatic.   *(2 marks)*

5 What figure of speech is used in the phrase 'blackened and burnt
   and bare-headed'? (line 18)   *(1 mark)*

6 Read lines 27–33. Explain in your own words TWO reasons why
   fires were sometimes started deliberately.   *(2 marks)*

7 'There were too many people now.' (line 36)
   Why do you think this fact would make large bush fires less likely
   to happen?   *(2 marks)*

8 Looking carefully at all the evidence given in lines 37–46, explain to what extent Grandpa Tanner was afraid of fire. *(3 marks)*

9 The author's choice of language in the first sentence of paragraph six (lines 47–55) builds up suspense. Choose TWO words or phrases as examples and comment on each. *(2 marks)*

10 'Like a thousand locomotives steaming abreast.' (lines 51–52)
    a) What figure of speech does the writer use here? *(1 mark)*
    b) Explain why it is effective in describing the fire. *(1 mark)*

11 In paragraph six, the writer describes some of the dramatic effects of a bush fire. Which one of these do you find most amazing? Explain why. *(2 marks)*

12 Explain how the last two sentences make an effective ending to this extract. *(2 marks)*

TOTAL MARKS: 25

Taking a closer look (1) . . .

Personification

'It was an evil wind . . .' (lines 5–6)

One technique which Ivan Southall uses in this extract is **personification**. This is a figure of speech where something is treated as if it were alive. 'Evil' suggests that the wind has a mind of its own and is deliberately wicked.

We are told the smoke was 'teasing' Grandpa Tanner's nostrils. This gives the impression it is playing with him, trying to scare him, perhaps.

Personification helps to make writing more vivid and exciting.

For Practice (1)

Look at the first sentence in paragraph four (lines 26–27).

Pick out TWO words and expressions which suggest the smoke is alive.

Then try to explain what impression each of your examples creates of the smoke.

For Practice (2)

The following paragraph fills in some details about old Grandpa Tanner's family life and circumstances. Pick out THREE examples of personification from it. Say exactly what the author achieves in each individual example. Then try to say what the overall effect is, and how it affects our feelings for the character of Grandpa Tanner.

> There had been a time when he had been up around dawn almost every day, but there was no need for that now. His family had long since grown up and gone away; his wife Marjorie had been dead for so many years; the relentless bush had reclaimed his once splendid farm; dogwood scrub and blackberries had choked his fruit trees; sorrel and couch grass had overrun his garden; there was no cow to milk or hens to feed. The milkman called these days and Grandpa Tanner bought his eggs at the grocer's shop. There was not much left for Grandpa, really, except the routine of getting up and of going to bed, and remembering.

Taking a closer look (2) . . .

Fact or Fiction?

Ash Road is a work of **fiction**. This means it was completely made up by the author. Ivan Southall has invented the **characters**, the people in the story, and the **setting**, the area where his story takes place.

Newspapers report facts. The following article was published in *The Scotsman* newspaper on Monday, 20th January, 2003. It tells of very similar events which really happened around that date in Canberra, the capital city of Australia.

The style of newspaper reporting is different from that of a novel like *Ash Road*.

For Practice

Read the newspaper article and then answer the questions. You could do this exercise in groups or pairs.

Four left dead as bush fires ravage city

JOHN INNES

HUNDREDS of people in Canberra sifted through the charred remains of their burnt-out homes today, after the worst bush fires in the history of the Australian capital left four dead and thousands homeless.

The raging fires forced mass evacuation and destroyed at least 388 homes.

Hospitals treated about 240 people for burns and the effects of smoke from the fires that hit Canberra on Saturday. Many were residents who battled flames with garden hoses and buckets filled from swimming pools.

Fire crews said they were overwhelmed by the ferocity and magnitude of the flames. "I have been to a lot of bush-fire scenes in Australia ... but this is by far the worst," said John Howard, the prime minister.

Police said a 61-year-old man died of smoke inhalation while trying to save his house, and an 83-year-old woman died in her home. A 37-year-old woman was found dead at her bunt-out home, along with an unidentified body.

Officials said all fires had been contained, but some areas were still smouldering. There were fears that strong winds forecast for Monday could re-ignite the crisis.

Police patrolled charred and deserted neighbourhoods following isolated cases of looting and suspicions that some fires might have been lit deliberately.

At the height of the crisis on Saturday, when a state of emergency was called, fire-fighters called on people not to panic. Many residents reported no fire crews in their burning streets.

More than 20 per cent of the city was without power on Sunday morning and red-hot embers fell, sparking fears that more lives and homes could be lost.

A mist of fine ash blew through the streets and a thick pall of smoke hung over the city of about 320,000 people, which is surrounded by drought-hit farmland and tinder-dry forests. Strong, dry outback winds and soaring temperatures whipped up an inferno in its outer suburbs to the north, west and south, triggering unprecedented havoc on Saturday.

Mr Howard interrupted his summer holiday to tour the fire-scorched suburbs, where one resident told him of the speed of the fire.

"We just got a few precious things out and the family dog and within two minutes the house was just gone," Tony Walter told him.

Questions

1 Look at the headline.
   a) Explain the meaning of 'ravage'.
   b) Write down THREE pieces of information contained in the headline.

2 Find TWO examples of real places which are mentioned in the article.

3 Write down THREE examples of statistics (numbers in figures) from the article.

4 Find TWO examples of interviews. Write down the first few words and say who was interviewed.

5 Write down ONE example of a person's age being given.

6 Write down TWO phrases which make the story sound dramatic and exciting.

Checklist for newspaper articles:

- Writing is set out in columns
- A headline is used instead of a title, and sometimes sub-headings too
- Real people and places are mentioned
- Many statistics are given
- Numbers are written in figures
- Paragraphs are quite short
- There are few similes and metaphors
- Dramatic language may be used
- People have been interviewed and their exact words are quoted
- Peoples' ages are often given

Chapter 13

The War of the Worlds

There are plenty of books and films based on the idea of alien creatures coming to the earth from another planet. One of the earliest stories of this type was published in 1898 by H G Wells, a novelist who originally trained as a scientist. The story starts with a strange cylinder landing on the outskirts of London. It attracts a crowd of curious onlookers. Suddenly, the top begins to unscrew and a creature comes out . . .

1   I think everyone expected to see a man emerge – possibly
something a little unlike us terrestrial men, but in all essentials a
man. I know I did. But, looking, I presently saw something
stirring within the shadow – greyish billowy movements, one
5   above another, and then two luminous discs like eyes. Then
something resembling a little grey snake, about the thickness of a
walking-stick, coiled up out of the writhing middle, and wriggled
in the air towards me – and then another.

    A sudden chill came over me. There was a loud shriek from a
10 woman behind. I half turned, keeping my eyes fixed upon the
cylinder still, from which other tentacles were now projecting,
and began pushing my way back from the edge of the pit. I saw
astonishment giving place to horror on the faces of the people
about me. I heard inarticulate exclamations on all sides. There
15 was a general movement backward. I saw the shopman struggling
still on the edge of the pit. I found myself alone, and saw the
people on the other side of the pit running off. I looked again at
the cylinder and ungovernable terror gripped me. I stood petrified
and staring.

20   A big greyish, rounded bulk, the size, perhaps, of a bear, was
rising slowly and painfully out of the cylinder. As it bulged up
and caught the light, it glistened like wet leather. Two large
dark-coloured eyes were regarding me steadfastly. It was rounded,
and had, one might say, a face. There was a mouth under the
25 eyes, the brim of which quivered and panted, and dropped
saliva. The body heaved and pulsated convulsively. A kind of
tentacle gripped the edge of the cylinder and another swayed in
the air.

    Those who have never seen a living Martian can scarcely
30 imagine the strange horror of their appearance. The peculiar V-
shaped mouth with its pointed upper lip, the absence of eyebrow
ridges, the absence of a chin beneath the wedge-like lower lip, the
incessant quivering of the mouth, the endless mass of tentacles,
the deep breathing of the lungs in a strange atmosphere – above
35 all, the extraordinary intensity of the immense eyes – culminated
in an effect similar to nausea. There was something fungus-like in

Extract continued

the oily brown skin. Even at this first encounter, this first glimpse, I was overcome with disgust and dread.

Suddenly the monster vanished. It had toppled over the brim of the cylinder and fallen into the pit, with a thud like the fall of
40 a great mass of leather. I heard it give a peculiar thick cry, and immediately another of these creatures appeared darkly in the deep shadow of the aperture.

At that my terror passed away. I turned and, running madly, made for the first group of trees, perhaps a hundred yards away;
45 but I ran slantingly and stumbling, for I could not avert my face from these things.

There, among some young pine-trees and furze-bushes, I stopped, panting, and awaited further developments. The common round the sand-pits was dotted with people, standing,
50 like myself, in a half-fascinated terror, staring at these creatures. And then, with a renewed horror, I saw a round, black object bobbing up and down on the edge of the pit. It was the head of the shopman who had fallen in, but showing as a little black object against the hot western sky. Now he got his shoulder and
55 knee up, and again he seemed to slip back until only his head was visible. Suddenly he vanished, and I could have fancied a faint shriek had reached me. I had a momentary impulse to go back and help him that my fears overruled.

Questions

1 Look at paragraph two.
  Write down three individual words or short phrases which suggest the feeling of fear. *(3 marks)*

2 Look at paragraph three.
  a) State two features of the Martian creature that resemble humans. *(2 marks)*
  b) Name one way in which it did not resemble a human.
  (1 mark)

3 Look at lines 23 to 24.
   What effect does the expression 'one might say' have on the
   meaning of the sentence?   *(1 mark)*

4 In the first three paragraphs the main feeling is fear. In paragraph
   four, the writer is 'overcome with disgust and dread'.
   List four features of the creature that made the writer feel this way.
   (You may quote).   *(4 marks)*

5 Look at the sentence beginning 'The peculiar V-shaped mouth'
   (line 30) and ending in 'similar to nausea' (line 36)?
   a) What do you notice about the punctuation of this sentence?
                                                               (1 mark)
   b) Why do you think the writer keeps the phrase 'culminated in
       an effect similar to nausea' at the end of the sentence?
                                                               (1 mark)
   c) Rewrite this phrase in simpler language.   *(2 marks)*

6 Look at paragraph five. (lines 38–42)
   Why did the monster disappear from view?   *(2 marks)*

7 What did the narrator do next?   *(2 marks)*

8 The crowd of onlookers felt both interested in and frightened by
   the creature. Quote a phrase which suggests that they felt this way.
                                                               (1 mark)

9 Throughout this extract, the writer carefully selects descriptive
   words and comparisons to make the creature sound as unpleasant
   as possible. Find at least three different examples of this use of
   language and discuss how effective you find these.   *(5 marks)*

TOTAL MARKS: 25

Strange but true . . .

RADIO LISTENERS IN PANIC

Many Flee Homes to Escape 'Gas Raid From Mars'

That headline actually appeared in a New York newspaper on 31 October 1938.

The night before, a radio dramatisation of H G Wells' *The War of the Worlds* had been broadcast, starring actor Orson Welles.

The setting of the story had been changed from London to New Jersey. The programme was so realistic that people thought the invasion was really happening! Hundreds of people fled from their homes to seek shelter elsewhere, and the police were swamped with phone calls from terrified members of the public.

Taking a Closer Look . . .

Words and their Meanings

A copy of H G Wells' description of the Martian creature was sent back to the authorities on Mars.

However, the Martians had some difficulty in understanding some of the words used.

Help them match up the following words with the correct definitions.

incessant	to move in and out regularly
nausea	a strong urge to do something
tedious	glowing in the dark
pulsate	sparkled and shone
inarticulate	continuing without stopping
luminous	boring, lasting for a long time
terrestrial	sticking out at the edge
projecting	feeling of sickness
glistened	unable to express yourself clearly in words
impulse	belonging to the earth

For Further Study

Further exercises on **Vocabulary** can be found in *Knowledge About Language*, pages 115–116

Chapter 14

The Lost Continent

In a recent poll, Bill Bryson was voted the most popular contemporary author in Britain. He has lived in both Britain and the USA, and he has also visited Europe, Australia and Africa. His accounts of his travels are very personal and amusing. Bill Bryson was brought up in Des Moines, the state capital of Iowa in the Midwest of America, where life is old-fashioned in some ways. **The Lost Continent** is an account of a journey around the United States which he made on returning to his homeland after living abroad for some time.

Extract

1   My father liked Iowa. He lived his whole life in the state, and is even now working his way through eternity there, in Glendale Cemetery in Des Moines. But every year he became seized with a quietly maniacal urge to get out of the state and go on vacation.
5   Every summer, without a whole lot of notice, he would load the car to groaning, hurry us into it, take off to some distant point, return to get his wallet after having driven almost to the next state, and take off again for some distant point. Every year it was the same. Every year it was awful.

$\rightarrow$

10   On vacations, my father was a man obsessed. His principal obsession was with trying to economise. He always took us to the crummiest hotels and motor lodges, and to the kind of roadside eating-houses where they only washed the dishes weekly. You always knew, with a sense of doom, that at some point before
15   finishing you were going to discover someone else's congealed egg-yolk lurking somewhere on your plate or plugged between the tines of your fork. This, of course, meant cooties[1] and a long, painful death.

But even that was a relative treat. Usually we were forced to
20   picnic by the side of the road. My father had an instinct for picking bad picnic sites – on the apron[2] of a busy truck stop or in a little park that turned out to be in the heart of some seriously deprived ghetto, so that groups of children would come and stand silently by our table and watch us eating – and it always became incredibly windy
25   the moment we stopped, so that my mother spent the whole of lunchtime chasing paper plates over an area of about an acre.

In 1957 my father invested $19.98 in a portable gas stove that took an hour to assemble before each use and was so
30   wildly temperamental that we children were always ordered to stand well back when it was being lit. This always proved
35   unnecessary, however, because the stove would flicker to life only for a few seconds before puttering out, and my father  would spend many hours turning it this way and that to keep it
40   out of the wind, simultaneously addressing it in a low agitated tone normally associated with the chronically insane.

All the while my brother, sister and I would implore him to take us some place with air-conditioning, linen table-cloths and ice-cubes clinking in glasses of clear water. 'Dad,' we would beg,
45   'you're a successful man. You make a good living. Take us to a

Howard Johnson's'[3]. But he wouldn't have it. He was a child of the Depression[4] and where capital outlays were involved he always wore the haunted look of a fugitive who had just heard bloodhounds in the distance.

50   Eventually, with the sun low in the sky, he would hand us hamburgers that were cold and raw and smelled of butane. We would take one bite and refuse to eat any more. So my father would lose his temper and throw everything into the car and drive us at high speed to some roadside diner. And afterwards, in

55 a silent car filled with bitterness and unquenched basic needs, we would mistakenly turn off the main highway and get lost and end up in some no-hope hamlet with a name like Draino, Indiana, or Tapwater, Missouri, and get a room in the only hotel in town, the sort of rundown place where if you wanted to watch TV it meant

60 you had to sit in the lobby and share a cracked leatherette sofa with an old man with big sweat circles under his arms. The old man would almost certainly have only one leg and probably one other truly arresting deficiency, like no nose or a caved-in forehead, which meant that although you were sincerely intent

65 on watching *Laramie*[5], you found your gaze being drawn, ineluctably and sneakily, to the amazing catch-away body sitting beside you. You couldn't help yourself. Occasionally the man would turn out to have no tongue, in which case he would try to engage you in lively conversation. It was all most unsatisfying.

70   After a week or so of this kind of searing torment, we would fetch up at some blue and glinting sweep of lake or sea in a bowl of pine-clad mountains, a place full of swings and amusements and the gay shrieks of children splashing in water, and it would all almost be worth it. Dad would become funny and warm and even once or

75 twice might take us out to the sort of restaurant where you didn't have to watch your food being cooked and where the glass of water they served you wasn't autographed with lipstick. This was living.

[1] cooties: lice
[2] apron: tarmacked parking area
[3] Howard Johnson's: chain of roadside restaurants which serve good food
[4] Depression: period of economic hardship and unemployment in the 1930s
[5] *Laramie*: a TV series of Westerns popular in the 1960s

Questions

1 Explain simply what Bryson means when he says his father is 'working his way through eternity' in Glendale Cemetery. *(1 mark)*

2 Explain two clues from the first paragraph which show the author's father was quite disorganised. *(2 marks)*

3 a) What is the meaning of 'economise' (line 11)? *(1 mark)*
   b) Pick out the information from the rest of the paragraph which helps to make the meaning of 'economise' clear. *(1 mark)*

4 Which of the following is closest in meaning to the phrase 'a relative treat' (line 19):
(i) a very enjoyable occasion;
(ii) reasonably nice compared with some other things;
(iii) something special to do with relatives. *(1 mark)*

5 Explain in your own words the problems with ONE of the picnic sites his father chose. *(2 marks)*

6 What reason did the Bryson children give to their father that he should take them to a good restaurant? *(2 marks)*

7 Explain clearly in your own words what is meant by the expression 'a child of the Depression' (lines 46–47). *(2 marks)*

8 How does the comparison Bryson uses in lines 48–49 help to illustrate how much his father hated spending money? *(2 marks)*

9 Explain the effect of the expression 'puttering out' (line 38) compared with simply 'going out.' *(1 mark)*

10 Read the opening sentence of the second last paragraph (lines 50–51)

Show how the author uses word order to emphasise how slow the camping stove was. *(2 marks)*

11 Bryson has invented the names 'Draino' and 'Tapwater' in lines 57–58. What impression do these names give of such American small towns?   *(2 marks)*

12 Explain how the context (the other information and ideas in the paragraph) helps you to understand the meaning of the word 'deficiency' (line 63).   *(2 marks)*

13 Read the last paragraph again. Pick out TWO descriptive phrases which are very appealing. Explain separately why each of them has this appealing effect.   *(4 marks)*

TOTAL MARKS: 25

Taking a closer look . . .

Hyperbole

Bill Bryson uses several techniques to make his writing humorous. One of the main ones is **hyperbole**, or exaggeration.

For example, in the first paragraph he says that his father would always forget his wallet, and have to go back for it 'after having driven almost to the next state.' Since states in America are hundreds of miles in extent, it seems that this is an exaggeration – in reality, his father perhaps once or twice had to drive back one or two streets to collect something.

Every paragraph in the story contains at least one example of hyperbole.

For Practice

Divide into groups, each group looking at one paragraph of the story.

1 a) Pick out all the examples of hyperbole you can find.

   b) Decide what you think might have *actually* happened.

2 Report back your findings to the rest of the class.

3 Individually, try writing a short paragraph about a car trip in the style of Bill Bryson, using one or two examples of hyperbole.

Chapter 15

Bee Season

Bee Season by Myla Goldberg takes its title from a spelling competition called a 'bee'. It is the story of an eleven-year-old American girl called Eliza who is in a low stream at school and feels she is inferior to her clever brother, Aaron, and a disappointment to her father, Saul. She believes she is not popular, attractive or talented.

However, one day she discovers she is amazingly good at spelling. She is astonished when she wins a school spelling competition. After winning this, she goes forward as her school representative in a district competition.

Extract

1   When Eliza arrives home, Saul's first thought is how nice it is that the district bee gives away such huge consolation trophies. It takes him a few
5   moments of hearing his daughter's "*I won! I won!*" and feeling her arms wrapped around his waist to comprehend that the trophy is no consolation. He scoops his little girl
10   into his arms and tries to hold her above his head but realises, midway, that he hasn't tried to do this for at least five or six years. He puts her back down, silently resolving to start exercising.

"Elly, that's fantastic! I wish I could have been there. I bet it
15   was something else, huh, Aaron?"

Aaron smiles and nods, tries to think of what a good older brother would say. "She beat a lot of kids, Dad. You would have loved it."

"I know, I know. And I didn't even think to give you the camera." Saul shakes his head. "But now I get another chance. You're going on to the next level, right?"

Eliza nods. "The area finals are in a month. In Philadelphia."

Saul claps his hands. "Perfect! We'll all go. A family trip. A month should give your mother enough time to clear the day. I'm so proud of you, Elly. I knew it was just a matter of time until you showed your stuff. A month. I can barely wait."

At which point Eliza realises that she has only four weeks in which to study.

Studying has always been a chore on the level of dish-washing and room-cleaning, approached with the same sense of distraction and reluctance. The days following her spelling win, she resolutely maintains her after-school schedule of television reruns[1], pretends not to notice her father's raised eyebrows at the sight of her in her regular chair, without a spelling list or dictionary in sight. More than her father's unspoken expectations, it is Eliza's growing suspicion that she has stumbled upon a skill that convinces her to take out the word lists. She realises she has never been naturally good enough at anything to want to get better before. She renames studying "practice". Spelling is her new instrument, the upcoming bee the concert for which she must prepare her part. Eliza knows that something special is going on. On Wednesday, she remembers the words she studied on Monday and Tuesday. On Thursday, she remembers all the old words, plus the new ones from the day before. The letters are magnets, her brain a refrigerator door.

Eliza finally understands why people enjoy entering talent shows or performing in recitals. She stops hating Betsy Hurley for only doing double-Dutch jump rope at recess. If Eliza could, she would spell all the time. She starts secretly spelling the longer words from Ms Bergermeyer's droning class lessons and from the nightly TV news broadcasts. When Eliza closes her eyes to spell, the inside of her head becomes an ocean of consonants and vowels, swirling and crashing in huge waves of letters until the word she wants begins to rise to the surface. The word spins and

Extract continued

55 bounces. It pulls up new letters and throws back old ones, a
fisherman sorting his catch until it is perfectly complete.

Eliza can sense herself changing. She has often felt that her
outsides were too dull for her insides, that deep within her there
was something better than what everyone else could see. Perhaps,
60 like the donkey in her favourite bedtime story, she has been
turned into a stone. Perhaps, if she could only find a magic
pebble, she could change. Walking home from school, Eliza has
often looked for a pebble red and round, that might transform
her from her unremarkable self. When Eliza finds this pebble in
65 her dreams, her name becomes the first the teacher memorises at
the beginning of the school year. She becomes someone who gets
called to come over during Red Rover, Red Rover, someone for
whom a place in the lunch line is saved to guarantee a piece of
chocolate cake. In the dream, Eliza goes to sleep with this magic
70 pebble under her head. The dream is so real that she wakes up
reaching beneath her pillow. Her sense of loss doesn't fade no
matter how many times she finds nothing there.

After a week of studying, Eliza begins sleeping with a word list
under her head. In the morning it is always there, waiting.

¹ reruns : repeated programmes

Questions

1 At first, Eliza's father, Saul, thinks her prize is a 'consolation trophy'.
   a) Explain in your own words what is meant by a 'consolation'
      trophy.   *(1 mark)*
   b) What does Saul's first thought tell us of his opinion of his
      daughter's ability?   *(1 mark)*

2 Explain one piece of evidence from the first paragraph which
   shows it has been a long time since Saul has paid much attention
   to Eliza or praised her for anything.   *(2 marks)*

3 Find and explain an additional piece of evidence from lines 19–20
   which also shows that Saul had not expected Eliza to do well.
                                                                 (2 marks)

4 'At which point Eliza realises that she has only four weeks in which to study.' (lines 27–28)

Explain why the author has put this sentence in a paragraph by itself and what the effect of this is. *(2 marks)*

5 Explain how the comparisons to dishwashing and room cleaning in lines 29–30 help us understand Eliza's attitude to studying.

(2 marks)

6 Eliza pretends not to notice her father's raised eyebrows when she watches TV. Explain the signal you think his 'raised eyebrows' (line 33) give. *(1 mark)*

7 Read the whole paragraph beginning at line 29: 'Studying has always been a chore . . .'
Explain why Eliza does not mind studying when it is spelling she is working at. *(2 marks)*

8 'Spelling is her new instrument . . .' (lines 39–40)
Pick out TWO words in the rest of the sentence which continue the image of spelling as a musical instrument. *(2 marks)*

9 Read the paragraph beginning at line 46: 'Eliza finally understands . . .'
a) What does Eliza now understand about people who show off and why they do it? *(2 marks)*
b) Which word in this paragraph suggests Ms Bergermeyer is not a very good teacher? Explain what it means. *(2 marks)*

10 In the paragraph beginning 'Eliza can sense' (line 57) we learn that Eliza has a dream of finding a 'magic pebble' which will transform her.
a) Pick out the expression which suggests she believes she is nothing special. *(1 mark)*
b) In your own words, explain TWO things which Eliza believes might happen if she were magically to become popular.*(2 marks)*

11 Why do you think Eliza puts her word list under her pillow at night? In what way could her word list act like the 'magic pebble' of her dreams? *(3 marks)*

TOTAL MARKS: 25

For Further Study

More information and exercises on **Spelling** can be found in *Knowledge About Language,* pages 46–57

Taking a closer look (2) . . .

Spelling

For Practice (1)

The following list includes some of the words which Eliza had to spell in order to pass into higher rounds of the competition.

Look at them for five minutes. Ask someone to read the list to you, and see how many you get correct.

tomorrow	secretary
lizard	imminent
raspberry	possibility
weird	correspondent
canary	element

For Practice (2)

The letters of the following rather difficult spelling words have been scrambled. Can you work out how each work should be spelt? To help you know what the word is, an indication of the sound is given and there is also a definition of the word.

Cross out each letter in the scrambled word to check that you have included it.

Scrambled word	Sounds like	Means
hidlice	kayly	an evening of Scottish dancing
zedsouvner	rongdyvoo	meeting
aubure	byoorow	writing desk
ceusinna	nyoosins	something annoying
schoumisive	mischivis	naughty
eugga	gaje	measure
starturnea	restrong	café
matrepent	perminint	everlasting

Appendix 1: Further Revision and Practice

Word choice

Choosing one word instead of another can create a particular effect.

For example, consider the underlined words in these two sentences:

> Jim <u>plodded</u> along the road.
>
> Jim <u>walked</u> along the road.

In the first sentence think about the effect of 'plodded'. It makes Jim sound tired or depressed, or he might be carrying a heavy load. It might make you feel sorry for him.

'Walked' is a more neutral word. We cannot tell much about Jim from it, and it does not arouse any special feelings in the reader.

For Practice a)

Say what special meaning the underlined words have. A more neutral version is given in brackets so that you can compare them.

1 Jenny <u>clung</u> to her mother's hand. (Jenny held her mother's hand.)

2 Sandy <u>slouched</u> at his desk. (Sandy sat at his desk.)

3 Billy <u>rushed</u> outside. (Billy ran outside.)

4 The trapped man <u>eased</u> his legs from under the rubble. (The trapped man pulled his legs from under the rubble.)

5 John <u>wolfed</u> his dinner. (John ate his dinner.)

6 The soldiers <u>trudged</u> back to their billets. (The soldiers returned to their billets.)

7 Steven <u>stole</u> into the office. (Steven went into the office.)

8 A figure was <u>lurking</u> by the door. (A figure was standing by the door.)

9 Their leader <u>brandished</u> his sword. (Their leader held up his sword.)

10 Sally <u>whisked</u> the photograph away. (Sally put the photograph away.)

You might also think about whether a word is **simple** or **complex**. For example, 'house' is simple, while 'habitation' is complex. Sometimes a writer will aim to use simple words for a reason, such as to suggest the thoughts of a child. (See chapters 5 and 10, for example.)

For Practice b)

Make two columns headed like this.

Simple	Complex

Then write each of the words below in the appropriate column. The words are in pairs of similar meaning – one simple, another more complex.

Elementary / easy   hate / detestation   fear / apprehensiveness

delightful / nice   grand / impressive   departed / left

fun / entertainment   ascended / climbed   alike / indistinguishable

endeavour / try   perceive / see   kind / benevolent

You could also consider whether a word is **formal** or **informal**. When deciding this, think of whether you would feel comfortable *saying* it. For example 'Mum' is informal, and 'mother' is formal. A writer may use informal words when he is aiming to give the impression that someone is speaking.

For Practice c)

Make two columns headed like this.

Formal	Informal

Then write each word in the appropriate column. The words are in pairs of similar meaning – one formal, the other informal.

nosy / inquisitive   terrifying / scary   posh / aristocratic
acquaintance / pal

disturbed / crazy   Dad / father   cheeky / impertinent
unintelligent / dopey

brainy / intellectual   untrustworthy / sneaky

Word choice has many aspects, but the main thing to think about is what *effect* the word has on *you*.

Tip:

When you answer questions in a Close Reading test, you yourself should aim at using words which are **simple** and **formal**.

Figures of speech

Figures of speech are like decorations in language to make it more interesting.

The following five figures of speech which have already been looked at in this book are the commonest, and ones which you will learn to recognise.

The first three involve **comparisons**. Usually, the two things being compared will be alike in at least one obvious way such as colour or texture, but quite unlike in other ways.

Simile: this comparison always uses the word 'like' or 'as'. For example:

The grains of sand sparkled <u>like diamonds</u>.
Clouds, <u>white as feathers</u>, drifted overhead.

In the first example, we can easily picture the brightness and fire of diamonds, and this helps us imagine the beauty of clean, dry sand and its crystalline texture. In the second example, comparing the clouds to feathers helps us imagine very white, soft looking clouds.

Metaphor: this comparison does not use the word 'like' or 'as'. One thing is just said to *be* another. For example:

A <u>blizzard</u> of gulls followed the boat.

In this example, a flock of seagulls is compared to snowflakes. Gulls and snowflakes are alike in being white and flying around in the air. Picturing a snowstorm helps us imagine how very many gulls there are and how they swirl around in flight.

Personification: this is a kind of metaphor in which an object is spoken of as if it is alive. For example:

The car leapt forward with a roar.

A car is a machine controlled by its driver, but to say it 'leapt' makes it sound like an animal with a mind of its own, and 'roar' suggests it has a voice, too. These ideas help to give an impression of how powerful and even dangerous the car is.

These three figures of speech are known as **imagery**, and the things which are used for comparison (diamonds, feathers, blizzard etc.) are **images**.

Other figures of speech depend on the *sound* of the words.

Alliteration is the name given to the deliberate repetition of sounds at the beginning of words. This makes the expression stand out. For example:

'*the forest's ferny floor*'.

Try to think what *sort* of sound is used and what *effect* it has. In this example the sound 'f' is very soft, like a whisper. It creates an impression of the quiet, still depths of the forest.

Onomatopoeia is an easy figure of speech to recognise, though not to spell! It is the name given to the technique where the sound of a word imitates the meaning.

For example, words like *sizzle*, *bubble* and *mew* all sound like their meanings.

For Practice

Say which figure of speech is underlined in each example. Then discuss how effective each is. You could do the second task in groups, with each group selecting two or three examples to work on.

1 The law's <u>as tricky as a ten-foot snake</u>.
2 Pike, three inches long, <u>perfect pike in all parts</u>.
3 The <u>hissing</u> geese were a terror.

4   The sea is <u>a hungry dog</u>.

5   Lights <u>blinked</u> along the runway.

6   Her hair was <u>a gleaming helmet of copper</u>.

7   Hunger <u>stalked</u> through the land.

8   The scientist said the exploding bomb was '<u>as bright as a thousand suns</u>'.

9   The <u>whizz</u> of the Catherine wheel startled us.

10 'I heard the owl scream and the <u>crickets cry</u>,' said Lady Macbeth.

Sentence structure

Sentence structure is the name given to the way words are arranged in sentences. The patterns used may be very complex, but there are some simple things you can look for.

You might consider if the writer uses **questions** or **exclamations**, for example.

Are the sentences short and abrupt or do they seem long and drawn out?

Is there any **repetition**?

Is there anything unusual about the **order** of the words in the sentence?

The beginning and the end of the sentence are the **stress positions**, and words put there will be intended to stand out for some reason.

Does the writer make use of **direct speech**? Inverted commas will usually make this clear, although sometimes writers may mark it in other ways. (Look at Chapter 10. How does Roddy Doyle mark direct speech in the extract from *Paddy Clarke Ha ha ha*?)

Does the writer tell the story himself, using 'I'? This is known as using the **first person**.

Look carefully at the **punctuation marks**, and think about how they divide up the sentence.

Noticing techniques like these, and thinking about why they are used will help you understand the piece of writing more fully.

For Practice

Draw up your own checklist of things to look for in sentence structure questions. Make a list of bullet points.

Tone

When questions ask about 'tone', they want you to guess at the *feelings* the writer is aiming to put across. A good introduction to tone is to consider feelings as they are expressed in direct speech.

For example, 'Let me! Let me!' could be described as an *eager* tone or an *enthusiastic* tone.

Look at the extracts of direct speech following, and then try to match them up with the tones given.

1 "Please don't leave! Please!"

2 "How dare you!"

3 "I wonder who the visitor can be? Do you know?"

4 "Well done! That is a really great achievement!"

5 "I can't see any point in going on with this. It will never be any good."

6 "Don't worry. I'm sure everything will turn out all right in the end."

7 "Keep going! You can do it!"

8 "What a shame!"

---

a) Pitying

b) Angry / offended

c) Depressed / disheartened

d) Encouraging

e) Congratulating

f) Consoling

g) Curious / inquiring

h) Pleading

This will give you an idea of what is looked for in a tone question. Of course writers can also express a mood in other ways, such as through descriptive details of setting, for example.

Answers

Authors' Note

The following pages contain suggested answers and marking schemes for the Close Reading tests and the language exercises in the 'Taking a Closer Look' sections.

The answers reflect what the authors had in mind while setting the questions, but they should not be regarded as prescriptive in all cases. It is very likely that other valid responses may be offered and teachers should use their own judgement in allocating marks for these.

Mary M. Firth and Andrew G. Ralston
2003

Answers

Chapter 1: The Kingdom by the Sea

1 a) He was used to air raids / he was experienced / he knew what to do. *(1 mark)*

   b) He had left his clothes close at hand so that he could dress quickly.

     or

     References like 'his hands found his clothes' and 'all done by feel' show that he can carry out all the necessary actions automatically. *(2 marks)*

2 The lights might be seen by the bombers, thus helping them to identify targets. *(2 marks)*

3 a) Any four points from the following: a roll of blankets / wrapped in a waterproof cover / held together with a belt / a case containing a flask of coffee / insurance documents / brandy for medicinal purposes. *(4 marks)*

   b) Take them with him to the air raid shelter *(1 mark)*

   c) Blankets / coffee: to keep the occupants warm during the night. Brandy: in case anyone took ill or was injured. Insurance documents: in case the house was damaged or destroyed by bombing. *(2 marks)*

4 a) Because only one aircraft could be heard and because it was still far out to sea. *(2 marks)*

   b) Safe / comfortingly. *(1 mark)*

5 Any three of: deposited the equipment he was carrying on one of the bunks / located and lit the oil lamp / lit the candle / untied the bundle and spread out the blankets. *(3 marks)*

6 'Mam and Dad were taking their time tonight.' *(1 mark)*

7 The danger posed by the air raid was far greater than the likelihood of the house being broken into. *(2 marks)*

8 It emphasises Harry's growing sense of panic / desperation. *(2 marks)*

9 That the bombs had fallen on or near the shelter / that Harry had lost consciousness. (*Not* that he had died, as the passage says 'he remembered saying seven'.) *(2 marks)*

TOTAL MARKS: 25

Similes and metaphors

1, 2, 4, 5, 7 and 10 are similes; 3, 6, 8, 9, 11 and 12 are metaphors.

Chapter 2: Thimble Summer

1 'worst'. *(1 mark)*

2 The mercury in the thermometer (which is coloured red) had risen in the high temperatures. *(1 mark)*

3 a) simile. *(1 mark)*

 b) 'like a bright skin ... stretched tight' suggests the sky is like the skin of a drum; 'as though a great hand beat': thunder sounds like someone beating a drum. *(2 marks)*

4 There was no rain. *(1 mark)*

5 The crops were turning yellow; the leaves of the plants were dried up; the soil had turned to dust. (Any two) *(2 marks)*

6 The flat tone of the word 'Oh' with no other comment suggests she is unhappy or depressed. 'Turned back' tells us she hates the bills and does not want to think about them or even look at them. *(2 marks)*

7 The rhythm of the short words is effective as it suggests Garnet's movements in laying out the forks and knives one by one. The repetition indicates the repetitive nature of her chore of setting the table. The other expression would not do this. *(2 marks)*

8 Garnet enjoys it. 'Peacefully' suggests a pleasant calm atmosphere. 'Coolness' suggests relief from the heat upstairs. 'Knelt down and plunged both her arms into the water' suggests she is lingering there and enjoying the cold water. However, 'little shiver' suggests the water may be a little too cold for comfort. *(4 marks)*

9 Placing it in a paragraph by itself emphasises the sudden contrast in temperature from the 'cold room' to the hot kitchen. The simile 'like walking into a red-hot oven' is an exaggeration, but effectively suggests the blast of intense heat which Garnet feels when she walks in. *(2 marks)*

10 His words 'What a day' tell us he is depressed and has had a bad day. 'Shook his head' tells us he feels despair / unhappiness etc. *(2 marks)*

11 In temperature and in colour: it is warm and brown. *(2 marks)*

12 The sand bank where the thimble was found was normally under water, and had just emerged during the drought. *(1 mark)*

13 Garnet's excitement shows she is hopeful, optimistic and happy. Her belief in magic suggests she is innocent and naïve. Jay's words show he is more realistic and mature; he believes there 'is no such thing' as magic. He is calmer and less excitable; he seems more resigned to the hard times continuing. *(2 marks)*

Describing Words
For Practice (1)

1 torn; brittle

2 big; black

3 dark; quiet

4 brownish; lukewarm

5 rich; muddy

6 small; glittering, silver

For Practice (2)

hot – hotter – hottest

bad – worse – worst

bright – brighter – brightest

tall – taller – tallest

lively – livelier – liveliest

good – better – best

cold – colder – coldest

cool – cooler – coolest

Tone

1 angry. Clues: 'angrily'; 'shook her fist'.

2 despairing; depressed. Clues: negative words – 'No'; negative gesture – 'shook his head'.

3 happy / excited. Clues: 'triumphantly'; exclamation marks suggest joyfulness.

Chapter 3: The Cay

1 There was no warning or sound: 'silent'/ it was during the night / it was very dark: 'moonless'. *(1 mark)*

2 a) simile. *(1 mark)*

   b) Alike : both move underwater; they are both deadly;
   Unlike: sharks are living while submarines are machines / man-made. *(3 marks)*

3 They are short and wide. *(2 marks)*

4 They went on strike. *(1 mark)*

5 People had been proud at how important their islands were to the war and felt they were contributing to victory, but the strike was now hindering the effort and might cause defeat. *(2 marks)*

6 a) He believed the people who were criticising the Chinese sailors would not have risked their own lives to do the job / the Chinese sailors were being asked to risk their lives. *(1 mark)*

   b) He was open-minded and sympathetic to the feelings of others: 'they are very frightened'; he was understanding and could imagine what they were being asked to do: 'explained what it must feel like'; he was brave as he 'offered to help sail the tankers' despite knowing how dangerous it was and not being a sailor himself. *(3 marks)*

7 She did not like it as she was 'using the war as an excuse' to leave, suggesting she had wanted to leave even before the war. *(1 mark)*

8 They were tense and afraid because of the danger of an explosion from the oil fumes. *(2 marks)*

9 Many people turned out to watch, including the governor. There was great cheering as if at an important event. *(2 marks)*

10 Their morale was high as they were waving cheerfully and making v-for-victory signs showing their confidence. *(1 mark)*

11 A wall of red flames. *(1 mark)*

12 Philip stops seeing the war as a kind of adventure, being no longer 'excited', and instead sees the loss of life and damage it causes: 'death and destruction'. He is aware of how pointless the rescue attempts are: 'useless', and is disturbed by the sight of adults in tears, particularly men and even his own father. He finds it hard to believe that the great ship has gone: 'it didn't seem possible'. Philip is learning about life and the tragedies it contains: he had 'begun to understand'. *(4 marks)*

TOTAL MARKS: 25

Nouns
For Practice (1)

common	proper	abstract	collective
shark	Aruba	darkness	crew
house	Montgomery	gloom	
submarine		victory	
torpedo		defeat	
tanker		mutiny	
salt		excuse	
boat		voyage	
pilot		destruction	
water			

For Practice (2)

fewer	less
island	oil
night	petrol
refinery	gloom
defeat	water
bridge	salt
shell	food
sailor	rust
vegetable	smoke
day	
gun	
harbour	
motorboat	

Chapter 4: A Dog so Small

1 A letter, probably from his grandfather, giving details of how he would be able to get his dog. *(1 mark)*

2 a) He believed his grandfather had promised to give him a dog. *(1 mark)*

   b) He had not been given a firm promise (reference to/paraphrase of: 'his grandfather's promise had been only a whisper and a nod'; sometimes people break their promises ('not all promises are kept, anyway'). *(2 marks)*

3 It emphasizes Ben's disbelief / disappointment, etc. *(1 mark)*

4 When he discovered a parcel with his grandfather's writing on it, he realised that his grandparents had sent him something else instead. *(2 marks)*

5 a) With anger – he pushed it onto the floor. *(1 mark)*

   b) One of the following:
       Frankie and Paul: thought it was an unusual gift.

May and Dilys: liked it; thought it was attractive looking.
Mr Blewitt: showed little interest.
(1 mark)

6 The line 'and then he realised that they had sent him a dog after all' sheds light on Ben's feelings. What angered him was the fact that they thought a picture of a dog would be as acceptable to him as a real dog. He felt that his grandparents were almost mocking his desire to own a dog.
(2 marks)

7 Any well-expressed opinion which makes sense in the context of the rest of the passage. *(2 marks)*

8 Three points: (i) his granny valued the picture as it had been given to her by a close relative; (ii) it had sentimental value as the person who gave it to her had subsequently drowned; (iii) the fact that his granny was prepared to give Ben something she valued showed that this was a sincere act of generosity. *(3 marks)*

9 They were unable to afford one.
(1 mark)

10 (i) danger from traffic (ii) lack of a garden or park to exercise the dog in.
(2 marks)

11 Reference to 'he hated his father for being in the right' (line 73). Two feelings are (i) acknowledgement that his father's points were valid and (ii) frustration and anger at having to admit this to himself. *(2 marks)*

12 Possible references are 'eagerly' (line 13); 'the feeling that something might have gone wrong after all' (line 20); 'He knew for certain that something was wrong' (lines 25–26); 'He almost hated them for it.' (lines 37–38); 'Ben said nothing, because he could not' (line 55); 'he hated his father for being in the right' (line 73). Answers may also refer

to his action of sweeping the gift and wrappings onto the floor. *(4 marks)*

TOTAL MARKS: 25

Verbs

1 A verb is a doing word.

For practice a)

1 expected; 2 pushed; 3 glanced; 4 brought; 5 said.

For practice b)

1 sold; 2 read; 3 pushed; 4 picked; 5 assembled.

2 Words like 'be' and 'have' are also verbs.

For practice

1 climbed; 2 eat; 3 slept; 4 had, arrived; 5 hurry, shouted; 6 has, have; 7 frightened; 8 are, have; 9 scored; 10 is.

3 A verb can be made up of more than a single word.

For practice a)

1 am going, like; 2 have been trying; 3 have seen; 4 will be; 5 wonder, will beat.

For practice b)

1 might be going; 2 was being bullied; 3 will be going; 4 are looking; 5 has been working.

4 Verbs can be in different tenses.

For practice a)

VERB	TENSE
1 stopped	past
rested	past
2 looks	present
3 knew	past
was blazing	past
4 is	present
asked	past
5 will be	future
replied	past

121

For practice b)

wake, remember, need, sit, rub, feels, are stuck, is, is, are

Rewrite the passage in the past tense:

I woke up in a hot, dry wilderness. I remembered that we desperately needed water. I sat up and rubbed my grimy face with my hands and it felt like my eyelids and lips were stuck together. It was not far from dawn but there was none of the bright feel of sunrise in the air. The others were still fast asleep.

Chapter 5: When Hitler Stole Pink Rabbit

1 'Whispering' suggests Anna is not meant to hear and so might feel worried / Anna hears her father's name mentioned and will be upset in case something bad is being said about him / the 'Nazis' are mentioned who are enemies to the Jewish people. (Any one) *(1 mark)*

2 Their father had forbidden them to tell her; they were afraid the information might upset Anna. *(2 marks)*

3 Information that 1000 Marks reward was being offered for the capture of Anna's father; a photograph of her father. *(2 marks)*

4 a) Anna feels very alert and clear-headed. *(1 mark)*

b) Simile *(1 mark)*

5 a) She imagines her father in a room, going to bed. A shower of coins comes down from the ceiling and completely buries him. *(2 marks)*

b) She imagines her father is about to be killed in this way, or that he may even already be dead. *(2 marks)*

c) She had not just imagined it: it had been in the newspaper. *(1 mark)*

6 There was no postcard in the mail from her parents. *(1 mark)*

7 'Terror' suggests extreme fear; 'choked' suggests she herself feels suffocated with worry, as if she is going to die. *(2 marks)*

8 She is Jewish, and if she is afraid the Nazis will say all Jews are cowards. *(2 marks)*

9 It means that if anyone captures the person they will get a reward of money. *(2 marks)*

10 She doesn't want to be seen as foolish or weak / she does not want to worry her father / her fear now seems less important so she can laugh it off. *(2 marks)*

11 Anna's father is very brave, since he shows no fear that he is a 'wanted' man. He even makes a joke about it, ironically complaining his enemies are not offering enough money for him, showing he is very cool in the face of this threat. His humour is also evident when he jokes about writing to Hitler personally to complain. He is a good father, reassuring Anna by making light of the danger. *(4 marks)*

TOTAL MARKS: 25

Point of View
For Practice

1 Mama and Papa. These are Anna's names for her parents, and so we feel

we are seeing events through her eyes.

2 Anna is asking herself the question. She does not know the answer.

3 a) 'Silly' is a childish word; the sentence is very short and simple such as a child would use; her thought shows she does not understand the metaphor 'a price on his head' as she is just an innocent young girl.

b) determined.

4 Childish expressions like 'funny-looking' show it is a child's view; 'because it was in France' shows a child's comical view of a foreign country.

5

Anna thinking	Writer telling
a; d; e; g	b; c; f

Symbolism

'A price on his head'

a) Anna imagined that a shower of coins fell on her father and crushed him.

b) He would be killed.

c) The coins which kill him in the vision symbolise the money which someone will get for handing him over to the Nazis who will probably murder him. Indirectly, money will case his death, since he will be betrayed for it.

Chapter 6: A Series of Unfortunate Events

1 'initial opinion'. *(1 mark)*

2 a) a horrible person b) a depressing pigsty. *(2 marks)*

3 The dash introduces an elaboration of the previous statement, in this case an explanation of what the 'impressions' were. *(2 marks)*

4 It was very dirty and contained only one small bed. *(2 marks)*

5 They took turns sleeping in the bed, while the person not in the bed slept on the floor. *(2 marks)*

6 a) Violet *1 mark)*

b) She showed initiative in making a temporary bed out of the curtains. *(1 mark)*

7 The glass on the window was cracked; there was no cupboard or wardrobe to keep the children's clothes in, but only a large cardboard box; the paint or wallpaper was peeling off the walls/the room was poorly decorated. *(3 marks)*

8 Tolerated *(1 mark)*

9 'Demanding, short-tempered and bad-smelling'. *(3 marks)*

10 Any one of the following:

Demanding: always expecting the children to obey
Short-tempered: quick to become angry
Bad-smelling: smelt unpleasant
(1 mark)

11 That he was not always at home. *(1 mark)*

12 Repainting the back porch; repairing the windows. *(2 marks)*

13 Unsuitable – the tasks required skills children would not have; they were time-consuming, or any other similar reason. *(1 mark)*

14 The eye symbolises the fact that Count Olaf believed the children needed to be constantly spied upon as he did not trust them. *(1 mark)*

15 'As thick as thieves' (line 8).

(1 mark)

TOTAL MARKS: 25

Writing in Sentences (1)
For Practice (1)

Complete sentences:
Count Olaf's house was quite large.
Violet and Klaus took turns sleeping on the bed.
The sun streamed through the window.
Violet removed the curtains.
The house was a depressing pigsty.

Incomplete sentences:
Instead of toys, books or other things
Without curtains over the cracked glass
All over the house
If the people are interesting and kind
Your initial opinion on just about anything
Complete sentences make sense by themselves.

For Practice (2)

1 The orphans tried to get used to the house but they could not.

2 The early morning sunlight disturbed the children while they were still trying to sleep.

3 Violet made the curtains into a kind of cushion because the bed was very hard.

4 Klaus and Sunny soon became friends although they did not like each other at first.

5 The children felt very unhappy when Count Olaf came back home.

For practice (3)

1 After the children lost their parents they had to stay with Count Olaf.

2 When the children met Count Olaf they took an instant dislike to him.

3 Although Count Olaf's house was quite large, the three children had to share one room.

4 As Count Olaf did not want to do them himself, he left the children unpleasant jobs to do.

5 After Count Olaf had written a note to the children he drew a picture of an eye on it.

Chapter 7: Shoes were for Sunday (1)

1 Main points:
Mother had put Molly on window ledge while she cleared up.
Molly's foot caught on handle of the china bath.
Molly was distracted by sound of father coming in.
Both Molly and bath fell to the floor.
Bath smashed and Molly's nose was cut. *(4 marks)*

2 She squeezed her skin to stop the bleeding; grabbed hold of her, ran down the stairs and got onto a passing tramcar. *(2 marks)*

3 a) 'an edge cut through my nose like a knife'; 'spurting up like a well'; 'quick as lightning'; 'surefooted as mountain deer'. *(2 marks)*

b) Answer should stress what the two parts of the simile have in common: e.g. a constant flow of water from a well stresses how the bleeding did not stop. *(2 marks)*

4 'so impressed with his urgency'.

(1 mark)

5 The tram driver was prepared to deviate from the proper route of the

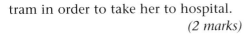

tram in order to take her to hospital.
(2 marks)

6 a) dramatic.

b) folklore.

c) extravagant. *(3 marks)*

7 They would place a halfpenny coin on the tram lines and wait until the tram ran over it. The weight of the tram was such that it would compress the coin so that it would look like a penny. *(2 marks)*

8 The children went dangerously near the trams without being in the least frightened. *(2 marks)*

9 'we saw little danger' OR 'surefooted as mountain deer'. *(1 mark)*

10 a) The drivers did not mind. *(1 mark)*

b) Paraphrase of 'they'd all played on the tramlines themselves when children'. *(1 mark)*

11 A guard at the front of the tram which could scoop up anything lying in its path to prevent it becoming lodged under the wheels. *(2 marks)*

TOTAL MARKS: 25

Genre
For practice

Genre	Title	Summary of Contents
Fantasy	*The Hobbit* by J R R Tolkien	The story of a magical adventure in Middle Earth and the quest for a powerful ring.
Crime	*Murder on the Orient Express* by Agatha Christie	Mystery about a passenger who is murdered on a train.
Biography	*The Hand of God: the life of Diego Maradona* by Jimmy Burns	The life of the famous Argentinian footballer who has been a key figure in four World Cups.
Autobiography	*Learning to Fly* by Victoria Beckham	The star tells the story of her life in the Spice Girls and her relationship with husband David.
Adventure	*Treasure Island* by R L Stevenson	The classic novel of pirates and treasure.
Travel	*Notes from a Small Island* by Bill Bryson	An American journalist journeys through the British Isles and writes about his impression of British life.
Science fiction	*The War of the Worlds* by H G Wells	A story about the invasion of the Earth by creatures from Mars.
Horror	*The Fall of the House of Usher* by Edgar Allan Poe	Gruesome story of a woman who is buried alive in the dungeons in an isolated mansion and who comes out of her grave.
War	*A Farewell to Arms* by Ernest Hemingway	The story of a love affair between a soldier and a nurse during the first world war.

Chapter 8: Shoes were for Sunday (2)

1 She wondered how anyone could be in the presence of an angel and not notice it. *(2 marks)*

2 'beautiful white wings' and 'clouds of glory round their heads'. *(2 marks)*

3 'angelic qualities could be found in the most unlikely guises'. *(1 mark)*

4 Answers should identify three features and explain these in different words.

Features might be 'little old lady' / 'roly-poly plumpness' / 'slightly bowed legs' / 'round rosy face' / 'grey hair caught up in an old-fashioned bun'.

Sample answer: She was a small elderly lady who was quite stout and had a round pink face. *(3 marks)*

5 She expected to start working as soon as she could in order to contribute to the cost of running the home. *(1 mark)*

6 She should go to college and gain qualifications / continue her education. *(1 mark)*

7 Children from working-class backgrounds rarely went to college in those days; it seemed an unrealistic / impractical / irrelevant idea (paraphrase of 'nothing to do with the business of living as we knew it'.) *(2 marks)*

8 Something that happened in stories but not in real life – i.e. a fantasy or dream. *(2 marks)*

9 She acted in a passionate / assertive / bossy / demanding way; she used a slang / American expression that was different from her usual style of speaking. *(2 marks)*

10 a) Any two of: letting Miss McKenzie down / not living up to her teacher's expectations / having to pay back the scholarship money if she failed. *(2 marks)*

   b) 'What if I fail her?' *(1 mark)*

11 Indomitable. *(1 mark)*

12 a) Miss McKenzie had given Molly chances in life that she would not otherwise have had. *(2 marks)*

   b) Recognition of the fact that the word 'door' is used metaphorically rather than literally. *(2 marks)*

13 Line 6: 'It never occurred to me that . . .'

Lines 61–62: 'And I knew for the first time . . .' *(1 mark)*

TOTAL MARKS: 25

Writing in Sentences (2)

For practice (a)

Statement: 2, 3, 5, 7
Command: 6, 8
Question: 1, 4, 9
Exclamation: 10

For practice (b)

1 First person:

Although I basked in Miss McKenzie's approval, I never really felt very close to her.

It never dawned on me to ask her advice as to what I should do when I left school.

Third person:

Miss McKenzie brushed all argument aside.

2 The extract belongs to the genre of autobiography. As Molly Weir is telling the story of her own life, a first person style is clearly appropriate.

Chapter 9: **On the Island**

1 a) Iain does not believe in them.

    b) Daial does believe in them.

                                (2 marks)

2 'I know people who have [seen a ghost]' or 'My father saw a ghost at the corner.' *(1 mark)*

3 a) Iain did not take Daial seriously.

                                (1 mark)

4 To go with him there and then to see if a ghost will appear. *(1 mark)*

5 'calm' / 'calm night'; 'they could feel their shoes creaking among the frost'.

                                (2 marks)

6 a) Iain likes reading b) Daial prefers fishing and football. *(2 marks)*

7 city. *(1 mark)*

8 Paraphrase of 'Iain in spite of his earlier protestations was getting a little frightened'. *(1 mark)*

9 They believed that people with second sight could foretell / predict that someone was going to die.

                                (2 marks)

10 Two of the following: Daial had become completely white / he had turned into a ghost / a skeleton.

                                (2 marks)

11 a) Possibilities include: 'he was a ghost who wished to destroy him' / 'Daial was a devil' / 'a corpse' / 'crazily' / 'frantic' / 'Daial was not Daial at all'. *(3 marks)*

    b) 'Iain's heart was beating like a hammer'. *(1 mark)*

12 As Daial had not seen the vision, Iain was frightened that his friend would think him a coward for running away.

                                (1 mark)

13

★ Iain tells Daial that he has seen a vision of a funeral procession

★ Iain says that he recognised that it was Daial in the coffin

★ He explains that there is no danger so long as the coffin does not touch the person

★ Iain begins to run, knowing that Daial will follow him

★ Daial is now grateful for Iain's action and cannot wait to tell the other boys

                                (4 marks)

14 Possible answers: 'Gosh, that's something' / 'You must have the second sight' / 'Wait till I tell the boys tomorrow'.

                                (1 mark)

TOTAL MARKS: 25

Direct Speech
For practice (1)

1 "I'll tell you something," said Daial to Iain.

2 "When are you going on your trip to Hong Kong?" asked Chris.

3 "I'm really looking forward to it!" said Tracy.

4 "I don't feel very well," complained Craig.

5 "How about a bite to eat at Burger King?" suggested my friend.

For practice (2)

1 The actual words spoken are enclosed in inverted commas.

2 The punctuation mark at the end of the actual spoken words comes inside the closing inverted commas.

3 When the actual words form a

question a question mark is used before the verb of speaking and the name of the speaker.

4 When the actual words form an exclamation an exclamation mark is used before the verb of speaking and the name of the speaker.

5 When the actual words form a statement a comma is used before the verb of speaking and the name of the speaker.

6 When there is a change of speaker you should begin a new paragraph.

7 If the same speaker continues after the verb of speaking and the name of the speaker you should continue in the same line.

For practice (3)

"According to this newspaper report," said Lewis, "Jack has been the most popular

boys' name for the last eight years running."

"I thought it would have been John," said Emily.

"It used to be," replied Lewis, "but John is now only number 62 on the list of the top hundred names."

"What's the most popular girls' name?" asked Emily.

"It's Chloe," answered Lewis, "but I don't know any girls called that."

"I do," said Emily. "There are two in my class at school. Where does all this stuff about names come from anyway?" she added.

"It says here," explained Lewis, "that it's based on a survey of the names given to 160,000 babies born in Britain during the last twelve months."

Chapter 10: Paddy Clarke Ha Ha Ha

1 They seemed to have freedom to do what they liked. *(1 mark)*

2 They climbed onto the back of the sofa and then jumped off it; they had mock sword fights ('duels') while sitting on the back of it. *(2 marks)*

3 He did not say anything; he just took what he wanted from the cupboard and closed the door again. Paddy would have expected Mr O'Connell to be angry and to be ordered out, but Mr O'Connell let him stay and even offered him a biscuit. *(2 marks)*

4 'Cut with a little lawn-mower' suggests a pattern formed by carving the surface of the material; 'felt like stiff grass' suggests the slightly abrasive bristly surface of the sofa cover. *(4 marks)*

5 He was used to his own parents or other adults telling him to go outside or reprimanding him. *(1 mark)*

6 a) Paddy felt disturbed by the lack of a mother figure; he felt a mother or father should be at the head of the table in charge of things. *(2 marks)*

   b) He uses a single paragraph for the one sentence. It has impact because it is so short. The simple monosyllabic words also have impact. *(1 mark)*

7 a) Crisps. *(1 mark)*

   b) 'all I ever had . . .' *(1 mark)*

8 The sandwiches piling up inside his desk started forcing his inkwell up. *(1 mark)*

9 Their teacher. He is in charge of them and gives orders to the boys. *(2 marks)*

10 Mould. *(1 mark)*

11 They are fascinated as they all watch; they are disgusted, as one of the boys is dared to eat the sandwiches. *(2 marks)*

12 He lets them eat out of a tin; he makes volcanoes out of the mashed potatoes; the food is bought rather than made at home. *(2 marks)*

13 She feels sorry for them. She says 'God love them', showing she feels it is sad they have to live on fish and chips as they have no mother to cook for them. *(2 marks)*

TOTAL MARKS: 25

Colloquial language

Feature	Example	Your examples
Abbreviations	It'd (short for 'it would')	Wouldn't; wasn't; couldn't etc.
Slang expressions	Yeah	Cool; scruffy; messing; etc
Use of first person	We were talking	Two of us; I liked ...' etc
Personal opinion/feelings	Messing on the sofa was great	I liked their house; they were brilliant etc.
Simple sentence structures	I liked their house	I didn't like that.
Simple expressions rather than more technical terms	One of these straw ones	Stuff was growing all over them.

Chapter 11: The Wind Singer

1 It was dark; it was ankle-deep in water. *(2 marks)*

2 There was a fast-flowing river running through it; there was a hole in the floor which the water fell through. *(2 marks)*

3 They were wet and slimy. *(1 mark)*

4 Although he was only their own age, he had white hair and wrinkled skin and walked slowly like an old person. *(2 marks)*

5 It sounded old and cracked like an old person's which made a frightening contrast with his child's body. *(2 marks)*

6 threatening; sinister. *(2 marks)*

7 They did not lift their feet and made a scuffing noise. *(1 mark)*

8 They did not seem hostile or likely to harm them but were just interested in them. *(2 marks)*

9 It made them feel weak, faint and sleepy. *(2 marks)*

10 'Crash and a splash' sounds like something fairly heavy and noisy, and perhaps clumsy; 'roared' suggests it is fierce like an animal; 'windmilling' suggests it is waving its arms and legs around and 'like a whirlwind' suggests something fast and strong. *(3 marks)*

11 She felt better as the cold water

revived her and brought her to her senses. *(1 mark)*

12 Kestrel is braver than Bowman. She is defiant: 'We're not going back', whereas Bowman 'shivered with fear'. In line 58, Bowman is so frightened that he asks Kestrel for help, and she defends him bravely: 'Get away from him'. Bowman is too scared to help Kestrel as he is 'immobilised by fear'. He 'did nothing' to help because of his fear, and 'felt shame'. Bowman is described as feeling 'sick with fear'. Kestrel is not scared when she falls in the water but keeps going. *(4 marks)*

13 The conversations in inverted commas are actually spoken; those in italics are communicated telepathically. *(1 mark)*

TOTAL MARKS: 25

Onomatopoeia

Word / Expression	Onomatopoeia
1 The match being struck	hiss
2 The lit torch hitting the ground	hissing
3 The lit torch hitting the ground	crackling
4 child's voice	husky
5 old children's feet	shuffling
6 laughter of children	rumbling
7 'something' charging out of the tunnel	splash
	crash
8 'something'	roared
9 heavy fall (which Kestrel expects)	smash
10 Kestrel landing in mud	plop; hiss

Chapter 12: Ash Road

1 a) He had smelt smoke. *(1 mark)*

   b) 'More than anything . . .' *(1 mark)*

2 It infuriated the men, it upset the women and scared the children. *(3 marks)*

3 The grass was very dry. It would catch fire easily. *(2 marks)*

4 'On his own' is repeated, showing how he had had to cope with a dangerous situation with no help; 'prayed' showed how desperate the situation was as he felt he needed God's help to survive. *(2 marks)*

5 Alliteration. *(1 mark)*

6 Farmers cleared ground / road workers tidied road verges / fire brigades cleared away fire hazards. *(2 marks)*

7 People would see them and report them before they got out of control;

help, such as fire services, would be closer at hand to put a stop to fires.

(2 marks)

8 He was not particularly afraid. He knew that fires, unlike some other natural disasters, could be controlled by experienced people; he himself had coped successfully with a fire before and saved his property. However, he was not complacent as he knew fires could be life-threatening and he personally knew some people who had died in them.

(3 marks)

9 'dreadful' is an emotive word which raises tension; repetition of 'the same' and in the phrase 'climbed and climbed' builds to a climax. *(2 marks)*

10 a) Simile. *(1 mark)*

   b) suggestion of huge size; immense power; masses of smoke etc.

(1 mark)

11 Examples: flying birds dropping dead; grass burning spontaneously; houses exploding; small rivers boiling. (Appropriate reason required.)

(2 marks)

12 They are short which makes them tense and dramatic. They are full of irony, since we suspect it *is* happening now. There is the effect of a cliff-hanger in Grandpa's sense of false security since we suspect the fire will be serious. *(2 marks)*

TOTAL MARKS: 25

Personification
For Practice (1)
Savage; on the rampage.

For Practice (2)
The <u>relentless</u> bush . . . <u>reclaimed</u>; blackberries had <u>choked</u> . . . couch grass had <u>overrun</u> . . .

Fact or Fiction
1 a) lay waste

   b) four people have died in the fire; there are major fires raging across the countryside; a city has had a lot of damage.

2 Canberra; Australia.

3 20% of the city has no power; 388 homes have been destroyed; 240 people were treated for burns and smoke inhalation; the city has 320,000 inhabitants.

4 John Howard, the Prime Minister: 'I have been . . .'

Tony Walter, a victim of the fire: 'We just got a few . . .'

5 A 61 year old man; an 83 year old woman; a 37 year old woman.

6 'raging fires'; 'battled flames'; 'whipped up an inferno'.

Chapter 13: The War of the Worlds

1 Any three of the following: sudden chill / loud shriek / horror / inarticulate exclamations / ungovernable terror / petrified and staring. *(3 marks)*

2 a) Any two of the following: eyes / face / mouth / saliva. *(2 marks)*

   b) One of the following: it was the size of a bear; it glistened like wet leather; heaved and pulsated; tentacles. *(1 mark)*

3 The expression suggests the creature had something vaguely resembling a face rather than a recognisable one. *(1 mark)*

4 Possibilities include: the shape of its mouth; the absence of eyebrows or chin; the sound of its breathing; the huge number of tentacles; its piercing stare; the texture of the skin (any four). *(4 marks)*

5 a) A list of features separated by commas. *(1 mark)*

   b) To achieve a climax. Rest of the sentence describes the features of the Martian while the last phrase describes how it affected the narrator. *(1 mark)*

   c) Culminated: built up to / reached a climax / ended with. Effect of nausea: made the viewer feel sick. *(2 marks)*

6 It had fallen over the edge of the cylinder and into the hole in the ground. *(2 marks)*

7 He ran away as quickly as he could, trying to reach the shelter of the trees; in his haste he could not run straight and frequently tripped.
(For two marks more is required than 'he ran away'.) *(2 marks)*

8 Half-fascinated terror. *(1 mark)*

9 Answers should include both quotations and comments on the effectiveness of these. Pupils should not repeat material used in earlier questions.

Unpleasant aspects of the creature include:

★ Its movements, which are emphasised in paragraph one (stirring, coiled, writhing, wriggled, etc).

★ Its texture (glistened like wet leather, fungus-like, oil skin, etc.)

★ Its features (many examples in paragraph four). *(5 marks)*

TOTAL MARKS: 25

Words and their meanings

incessant	continuing without stopping
nausea	feeling of sickness
tedious	boring, lasting for a long time
pulsate	to move in and out regularly
inarticulate	unable to express yourself clearly in words
luminous	glowing in the dark
terrestrial	belonging to the earth
projecting	sticking out at the edge
glistened	sparkled and shone
impulse	a strong urge to do something

Chapter 14: The Lost Continent

1 His father had died and was buried in Glendale Cemetery. *(1 mark)*

2 His father did not give them much warning about the holiday, but took off very suddenly; he often forgot something like his wallet and had to go back for it. *(2 marks)*

3 a) To save money / avoid spending money. *(1 mark)*

   b) He took the family to the cheapest hotels and restaurants he could find. *(1 mark)*

4 (ii) reasonably nice compared with some other things. *(1 mark)*

5 The place near a parking area for lorries and trucks would be noisy and dangerous; they would be embarrassed in the run-down city area by the poor children who would surround them looking for food. *(2 marks)*

6 He had a good job and he could afford it. *(2 marks)*

7 He had been young during the time of economic hardship in the 1930's (the Depression) and his attitude to money was shaped by this. *(2 marks)*

8 It is a comic exaggeration. An escaped prisoner would be terrified by being caught by bloodhounds on his trail, and this emphasises his father's absurd fear of spending money. *(2 marks)*

9 'Puttering' suggests it flickered for a while before finally going out, whereas 'going out' just says that the flame died without indicating how slow or fast this happened. *(1 mark)*

10 He uses inversion, delaying the subject 'he' till the middle of the sentence. He starts with two phrases indicating a long time, which draws out the sentence and emphasises the slowness of the procedure. *(2 marks)*

11 'Tapwater' sounds bland and dull; 'Draino' sounds dirty and unpleasant. *(2 marks)*

12 'Deficiency' means a lack of something. You can tell this since the man had one leg missing; an 'other' deficiency might be 'no nose'. *(2 marks)*

13 Suitable phrases for comment: 'blue and glinting sweep of lake or sea'; 'pine-clad mountains'; 'full of swings and amusements'; 'gay shrieks of children splashing in water'. *(4 marks)*

TOTAL MARKS: 25

Hyperbole

Possible examples:

Paragraph 1: a maniacal urge to get out of the state; load the car to groaning; return to get his wallet after having driven almost to the next state.

Paragraph 2: a man obsessed; they only washed the dishes weekly; a sense of doom; this meant cooties and a long, painful death.

Paragraph 3: on the apron of a busy truck stop; in the heart of some seriously deprived ghetto; spent the whole of lunchtime chasing paper plates; over an area of about an acre.

Paragraph 4: took an hour to assemble; my father would spend many hours; addressing it in a low agitated tone; normally associated with the chronically insane.

Paragraph 5: the haunted look of a fugitive who had just heard bloodhounds in the distance.

Paragraph 6: with the sun low in the sky; a silent car filled with bitterness; some no-hope hamlet with a name like Draino, Indiana or Tapwater, Missouri; an old man with . . . only one leg ; one other truly arresting deficiency like no nose or a caved-in forehead; the man would turn out to have no tongue.

Paragraph 7: searing torment; glass of water autographed with lipstick.

Chapter 15: Bee Season

1 a) A prize given to cheer up someone who has not won a competition. *(1 mark)*

b) He thinks she has little talent as he does not expect her to win. *(1 mark)*

2 He hasn't lifted her up in delight for five or six years; he calls her his 'little girl' as if he has barely noticed her growing up. *(2 marks)*

3 He didn't think of giving Aaron his camera, and therefore had not expected Eliza's performance to be worth marking with a photograph. *(2 marks)*

4 It makes it dramatic and shows Eliza's instant change of mood from being excited about winning the heat to suddenly realising what a lot of serious hard work lies ahead. *(2 marks)*

5 Dishwashing and room cleaning are dull, boring chores which children dislike, so we know that she does not enjoy studying and finds it tedious. *(2 marks)*

6 He disapproves of her watching television when she could be studying. *(1 mark)*

7 She is good at spelling and realises that she has the ability to get even better through study. This motivates her to work on it. *(2 marks)*

8 Concert; part. *(2 marks)*

9 a) She realises that they do have a special talent, and that doing something you are good at is very enjoyable. *(2 marks)*

b) 'Droning'. Speaking at length in a dull monotonous voice. *(2 marks)*

10 a) (her) unremarkable (self). *(1 mark)*

b) a teacher would learn her name first; / she would be picked first for games; / a place would be saved for her at the head of the lunch queue. *(2 marks)*

11 It is very precious to her, and may do wonderful things for her like the magic pebble would. Just like a magic pebble, her talent for spelling could change her life as her success would make her popular and happy.

(3 marks)

TOTAL MARKS: 25

Spelling

ceilidh
rendezvous
bureau
nuisance
mischievous
gauge
restaurant
permanent

Appendix 1: Further Revision and Practice

Word Choice
For Practice (a)

1 'Clung' suggests Jenny felt desperate and afraid and held on very tightly as if she would never let go.

2 Sandy sat down low and hunched up in his seat, as if he wanted to be invisible, or was bored, or wanted to look uncooperative.

3 'Rushed' suggests he ran out at high speed and with great urgency.

4 'Eased' suggests gently working his legs out as if they were painful, or in order to avoid dislodging more rubble.

5 'Wolfed' suggests eating very fast and hungrily, without attention to table manners.

6 'Trudged' suggests the soldiers were tired or in low spirits – it suggests a heavy tread.

7 'Stole' suggests he went furtively, trying not to be observed.

8 'Lurking' suggests the figure was up to no good, and makes it seem sinister.

9 'Brandished' is a confident aggressive movement, perhaps showing defiance or encouraging others.

10 'Whisked' suggests a very quick movement, as if she did not want people to see the photograph.

For Practice (b)

Simple	Complex
easy	elementary
hate	detestation
fear	apprehensiveness
nice	delightful
grand	impressive
left	departed
fun	entertainment
climbed	ascended
alike	indistinguishable
try	endeavour
see	perceive
kind	benevolent

For Practice (c)

Formal	Informal
inquisitive	nosy
terrifying	scary
aristocratic	posh
acquaintance	pal
disturbed	crazy
father	Dad
impertinent	cheeky
unintelligent	dopey
intellectual	brainy
untrustworthy	sneaky

Figures of Speech

1 Simile
2 Alliteration
3 Onomatopoeia
4 Metaphor
5 Personification
6 Mtaphor
7 Personification
8 Simile
9 Onomatopoeia
10 Alliteration

Tone

1 h) Pleading
2 b) Angry / offended
3 g) Curious / inquiring
4 e) Congratulating
5 c) Depressed / disheartened
6 f) Consoling
7 d) Encouraging
8 a) Pitying